Structured Strategic Partnership Handbook
A Practical Guide to Creating and Maintaining Strategic Partnerships that Add Value

The Association of Strategic Alliance Professionals (ASAP) has been a terrific partner by encouraging the development and distribution of this book.

More information about ASAP is available at:

Association of Strategic Alliance Professionals
960 Turnpike Street, Suite 3A
Canton, MA 02021
Tel: 781-562-1630
www.strategic-alliances.org

Structured Strategic Partnership Handbook
A Practical Guide to Creating and Maintaining Strategic Partnerships that Add Value

Ezra Schneier

Structured Strategic Partnership Handbook: *A Practical Guide to Creating and Maintaining Strategic Partnerships that Add Value*

Copyright © 2016 by Ezra Schneier

All rights reserved. This book or any portion thereof may not be reproduced or used in any manner whatsoever without the express written permission of the publisher except for the use of brief quotations in a book review or scholarly journal.

First Printing: 2016

This Version: 2020

ISBN 978-1-365-22466-9

Ezra Schneier

Dedication

To associates who create and manage Strategic Partnerships and Alliances.

It is hard yet gratifying work.

Contents

Acknowledgements xi

Preface xiii

Introduction 1

1. Why Do a Partnership? 4
2. Why Structure Matters 6
3. Structure Can Boost Performance 12
4. Outsourcing vs. Partnerships 17
5. Impact, Intimacy and Vision 19
6. Partnerships Can Lead to Acquisitions 22
7. Partnership Examples 26
8. Finding New Partners – Deconstruct Customers 30
9. Willing Partners 32
10. Alignment and Balance Are Critical for Success 35
11. The Structured Partnership Framework 37
12. State Your Goals 40
13. Profile of the Possible Partner 42
14. Presenting Structure to Partners 44
15. Presenting Structure to Your Internal Team 46
16. How to Choose the Right Partner 49
17. Sample Initial Partner Questionnaire 53

18.	Sales Projections Are Necessary from the Start	57
19.	Prioritize and Focus	59
20.	Proactively Reach Out to the Best Prospects	61
21.	The Business Case for a Partnership	63
22.	Reseller Arrangements	71
23.	Roll-Out – Introducing New Partnerships	76
24.	Sample Roll-Out Plan A	79
25.	Sample Roll-Out Plan B	83
26.	Sample Roll-Out Plan C	86
27.	Announcing a New Partnership	89
28.	News Releases about a New Partnership	91
29.	Segmenting the Audience for a Roll-Out	96
30.	Training	100
31.	Managing the Strategic Partnership	106
32.	Sample Strategic Partnership Project Plan	108
33.	How to Use Value Inflection Points	111
34.	Scorecard for Evaluating Partnerships	113
35.	User Conferences: The Partner Manager's Role	115
36.	Customer Lifecycle Communication	118
37.	Annual Audit of Partnerships	121
38.	Pricing, Compensation and Payments	125
39.	The Partnership Manager's Role	127
40.	Summary	131

41. Description of the Appendices...132

Appendix 1- Mutual Referral Agreement................................133

Appendix 2 – Referral Agreement - Unilateral......................142

Appendix 3- Mutual Confidentiality Agreement.................153

Appendix 4 – Sample Job Descriptions 160

Acknowledgements

Many professionals in the partnership world have contributed to the development of this book. Thank you for your thoughts and suggestions about how to bring more structure to partnerships and help us all improve and achieve greater success.

Partnerships are becoming more important for companies. They allow organizations to grow and deliver value to customers and stakeholders in today's changing business landscape. Having a process in place to select, introduce and manage those partnerships makes a difference in maximizing results.

The focus of this book is on bringing more structure to partnerships to achieve success. Of course, the goal of adding structure is to waste less time and resources and accomplish more. It is the fundamental premise here that structure is frequently a missing ingredient in choosing the right partnerships and making them work to their full potential.

Structure can be a guardrail to help keep an existing partnership on track. Structure works to assist in identifying the best partners in the first place and then successfully introducing a new partnership to the market.

Thanks for being on this journey.

Let's see what is possible.

Preface

Shortly after I started my first job in the Strategic Partnership arena, a colleague approached me and said, "You know the problem with Strategic Partnerships?" He continued by answering his own question: "They are not strategic and they are not partnerships. By the way, good luck."

I now know he was wrong. Strategic Partnerships can be both: strategic and real partnerships. But like most things, to be successful they have to be done right.

At the time, the company had a number of partnerships in place that were producing a fair amount of revenue and earnings. But no one really gave them much attention. There were two people managing them. These folks were never included in the main corporate dialogue or planning meetings. To say they were neglected would be an understatement.

This pair of colleagues loosely managed the partnerships. Mainly, they helped resolve service and billing questions. There was not a process in place to expand relationships with the existing partners or to introduce new partnerships to help foster additional growth. In short, there was no structure.

While this may not be the case in your company, there may be room for improvement in how your Strategic Partnerships are managed and viewed. Or, perhaps you want to identify potential new Strategic Partners to build or expand your organization.

With growth and achievement of goals in mind, additional structure may be a useful ingredient to propel your business. By including more structure, your partnerships may take a little longer to develop and manage. Usually, it is worth the effort. The resulting partnerships last longer and bring greater value. As much as we all like quick results, we know that structure can add time to our processes. But the value created warrants the extra time.

Adding structure takes hard work. While it is easy to find a few companies that say they want to partner and park their logos on your web site, the value from those partnerships is usually zero. What we are talking about here are real, enduring partnerships that add revenue, build customer loyalty and help companies get to the next level. It takes dedication and effort – and structure. As the old saying goes, "The hottest fire yields the strongest steel."

In this book are suggestions and tools we hope you find interesting and relevant to your situation and include in your playbook as a Partnership Manager. Maybe you can adapt one or two ideas presented here to add more structure and organization to your existing partnerships. As a result, these partnerships will be more sustainable. Accordingly, the value of partnerships, and the results they deliver to your business, can be enhanced.

Also, our goal here is to introduce ideas on how to create a blueprint to evaluate potential partnerships. Largely the objective is to select those partners that offer the most potential and can be most meaningful to your business. Above all, we hope you find this guide practical and helpful.

Introduction

Once considered a side dish for businesses, today partnerships are becoming prominent growth engines inside many companies. Strategic partnerships are becoming more vital to the expansion plans and competitive advantage of businesses.

In fact, as organizations race to expand and introduce new products and services, they seek out reliable partners who can help them deliver innovative solutions and expand market opportunities.

The value derived from the right partnerships can be huge. Partnerships can help fuel greater market share and give you a competitive advantage. They can increase revenue, lead to stronger customer loyalty and enhance financial performance.

Technology plays a part, too. For example, consider the growing availability of application programming interfaces (APIs.) This makes creating connectivity of services and solutions easier to develop than ever before. In turn, this can create a larger audience of potential partners and a broader service offering in the market. Clearly, advances in technology will continue to democratize opportunity, make interfaces faster and easier to accomplish - and partnerships more feasible.

In the manufacturing sector, technology allows a high degree of synchronization of the supply chain that can make partnerships attractive. Using technology available today, different companies can collaborate to dramatically reduce the time required to design, build, and test manufactured products.

Partnerships enable businesses to be more competitive and deliver what customers want. But if done poorly, partnerships can be a distraction. They can conflate different products or services that do not add value for either company or their customers. With structure we believe the distraction factor can be eliminated. Structure lets Partnership Managers keep long term plans clearly in focus and help maximize success.

What do we mean by "Structure?"

In the context of this book, we consider structure *Organized processes and standardized procedures for evaluating and managing partnerships.* Structure is a means to evaluate the actions and efforts being applied. Structure allows our efforts to be repeatable with stated goals and timelines. With a structured approach, our actions are put forth by design, instead of ad hoc. Each of the actions and efforts align with a well thought out plan and strategy. A good way to think of structure with partnerships is a process that is Measurable, Repeatable and Understandable.

Having a healthy dose of structure in your partnerships will help keep them active and fresh. When we speak with some business people about partnerships, we hear things like, *"They always seem to die on the vine."* With structure, we introduce a way to keep partnerships alive - and thrive.

Structure can be used in all phases of partnerships and alliances. We will supply a number of examples of structure in the hope that certain ones might be used in your situation. While we all may have different reasons for structure, they are generally firmly rooted in improved bottom line performance.

We create partnerships to add value. By their very nature, partnerships let us grow, reach new customers, build loyalty and increase revenue. Without question, this is an exciting time for those involved with partnerships. Best of all, this is just the beginning.

1. Why Do a Partnership?

Among the scenarios that may arise for seeking a strategic partnership with another company include:

- An executive in your company suggests finding partners who can sell your products and augment your direct sales efforts.

- Partners might be sought to fill certain product, service or capability gaps that you may have and level the playing field with competitors. (Or jump ahead of competitors in terms of offerings.)

- Customers might want you to develop a partnership with a particular company or type of company to round out the offering you supply.

- Gain a foothold in a particular industry or sector.

- Expand your operating footprint.

- Calls may be received from other companies asking you to explore a partnership. Sometimes this is a positive development. Other times, these inquiries should be decoded to mean "we want you to sell our products and services." Often, these folks do not want to take the time to figure out the real strategic fit and how value can be created. They want you to do work for them – bring them business. Usually they have little interest in how the partnership might benefit your business. (These discussions and relationships can be a drain on your resources. Having more structure in place will help reduce that drain.)

- A company in another market sector might want to develop a partnership to bring your product or service to their market and to their clients.

First, we will look at identifying and developing partnerships that can deliver value for both parties. This is the "choosing" phase and includes establishing key goals, such as generating more revenue and filling product gaps. It also involves vetting and prioritizing potential partners in a structured way.

Later, we will examine ways to introduce a new partnership to internal and external stakeholders. This is the "rollout" phase. The idea here is a lot of work goes into putting a strategic relationship in place, introducing the relationship and letting everyone know about it deserves ample thought and planning.

And we will discuss keeping the momentum going with partners: the "managing" phase. This is where we look at how to keep your partnerships growing - and not get stale. Sometimes, with existing partnerships we lose sight of their potential or even neglect them.

Naturally, like with all relationships, they require care and nurturing. In these pages we will discuss ways to keep partnerships top of mind and growing to achieve their full potential – and deliver success.

2. Why Structure Matters

It is the responsibility of a Partnership Manager to develop and drive the company's business strategy in the right direction through strong partnerships. Frequently, this includes growing existing partnerships along with developing and securing new relationships.

The role of the Partnership Manager is becoming more important to businesses. Partnership Managers have the power to change and grow organizations. Successful managers show they have a core competency doing partnerships without major missteps. This core competency puts them in high demand in today's market. Having a toolkit which contains elements of structure can help contribute to success for the Partnership Manager.

Partnerships and alliances are growing and becoming a greater priority for all types of businesses. In its 2015 Annual Survey of CEOs conducted by the prominent international accounting and consulting firm PwC a key finding was about the rapidly increasing gravity of strategic alliances:

Fast-tracking alliances to create new value

CEOs are designing the deal to complement the opportunity. In some cases, that means fast-tracking alliances to create value that a single company cannot achieve on its own. Businesses are actively participating in broad networks and seeking partners who are much more than alternative sales channels. Alliances today are built on finding the right companions—ones you can trust, whose values you share—to join together on a journey where the destination may not be predetermined.

With the growing importance of partnerships comes heightened attention to Partnership Managers or Strategic Alliance Specialists. Like all managers, the Partnership Manager or Specialist role requires prioritizing of available business opportunities and organizing resources. At the end of the day, the manager must make the partnerships which are in place work and bring real, measurable business results to the company. This may be in the form of increased revenue, market share, new customers and earnings growth. Usually, revenue – the mother's milk of business - gets the greatest attention and is most important.

Besides supporting the work needed with external partners, structure gives a Partnership Manager greater ability to maintain strong relationships with business unit leaders - *internal managers*. These internal relationships can make or break a partnership program. Managers in your company – and the teams they lead – are needed to drive awareness and adoption of partner products and execute the program. The Partnership Manager cannot do it alone.

Of course, internal managers are working fervently to run their departments and be leaders. It is critical for the Partnership Manager to be able to clearly show what is wanted from the internal manager and what they get in return. At risk of sounding cliché, it must be *win-win*.

Take the sales leader as an internal manager, for example. As the Partnership Manager you have identified a company with a fantastic product and are excited to introduce it to your clients. Adding a new product to your offering and telling prospects and clients about it requires sales to play an important role. But the sales leader is executing his sales plan and is busy helping his team achieve quota with the existing line-up of products. To introduce a new offering requires taking the sellers' time away from their routine to learn about a new product and how to sell it. Then there is a ramp-up period and the opportunity cost involved to consider. Time learning a new product takes away from selling what is already known. Understanding this challenge, the Partnership Manager can address it in several ways, such as:

a. Present the Sales Leader data about why the partner was chosen and the opportunity. If you have done your homework, you will be able to show that the chance of success is compelling.
b. Have suggestions about how to introduce the product. Maybe a segment of the market is addressed that does not have to involve the full sales team.
c. Develop and share sales and financial projections about the results the new product can bring to your company.
d. Show the support the partner company is bringing to the table. Maybe they are conducting training, bringing clients, funding part of the launch plan.

The important thing is for the Partnership Manager to have a structured approach to working with internal managers as well as external partners. This includes routinely explaining the value partnerships create for the organization and regular reporting on progress and results.

Having structure especially helps to bring internal awareness about partnerships and how they benefit your company. Then the elements of the program can be given the attention required. This can include technology, sales, marketing and other critical areas.

Structure contributes to scalability. The Partnership Manager wants to have repeatable processes so new partners can be identified and efficiently implemented. This allows for greater growth and capitalizing on consistent processes that work.

In our approach to bringing structure, we will look at three aspects, or phases, of strategic partnerships. These three pillars are:

- **Choosing** the right partners;

- **Roll-Out** - Introducing new partnerships in your organization;

- **Managing** and building partnerships to achieve your goals. This will include the practical everyday nurturing of the partnership to help it flourish and governance items that can help keep things going in the right direction.

As we examine each of these phases, suggestions will be made about how to add structure to your efforts to produce meaningful results. Central to this approach is the belief that structure can support your decision-making, bring success and drive improved results for your business.

Taken as a whole, the three phases of partnerships cover the full life cycle. You may have a desire to focus on just one of these areas for your business. As smart managers, we all try to identify ways to not just maintain our performance but to improve it. Perhaps you want to examine what you are doing in each phase and find ways to continuously build increased value.

Structure can be a hallmark of a successful partnership program and just as important as any of the other required ingredients. To this end, bringing structure into partnerships lets everyone know what is expected, clarifies the goals and helps keep the relationship on the desired trajectory.

Bottom Line: Why Structure Matters

- *Helps bring awareness and reinforcement about partnerships internally.*
- *Helps build commitment and support from internal managers.*
- *Keeps the value and goals of partnerships clearly in focus for internal managers and all stakeholders.*
- *Puts in place a method to flag problems and address them.*
- *Scalability. Allows for a standard framework that makes it possible to scale and repeat success.*

> - *Structure enables the Partnership Manager to efficiently accomplish strategic goals, such as growing and changing the business.*

3. Structure Can Boost Performance

Among the top reasons for introducing structure to partnerships:

- ✓ To produce greater results for your organization;
- ✓ To gain proficiency in the selection of partners and management of your relationships with partner organizations.
- ✓ To enhance productivity and reduce waste for the Partnership Manager and other involved parties.

Having structure provides a reliable and organized way to manage the business and planning processes needed for partnerships to succeed. This applies in each of the three main phases we will be examining: *Choosing, Roll-Out and Managing*. While each phase has its special attributes and requirements, introducing structure is additive for all stages.

A recent survey of members of the Association of Strategic Alliance Professionals (ASAP) focused on evaluating their alliances and what made them successful. Founded in 1998, ASAP is a non-profit global professional membership organization with over 2,500 members representing over 35 countries.

The survey of ASAP members was conducted in early 2015 and included managers and executives from high tech, Bio-Pharma and other industry sectors. Since the alliance business planning process is considered fundamental to the success of partnerships and alliances, it was chosen to be the heart of the study.

Results of the survey were published in a White Paper titled "*5th State of Alliance Study: Business Planning Processes.*" Its authors, Dave Luvison, Ard-Pieter de Man and Keith Gaylord, summarized the findings:

> Two-Thirds of the respondents indicated that their alliances were either meeting or exceeding expectations. However, it was considered curious that one-third of ASAP members' alliances would be underperforming. Three critical determinants of this difference were identified in the study:
>
> 1. Successful alliances had more formal processes for plan approval and dissemination to stakeholders. *Alliance managers should focus more effort on these processes.*
> 2. Successful alliances have greater involvement of high-level executives in the planning and actual results review processes. Additionally, when actual results were mutually reviewed with the partner, alliances performed better. *Alliance managers should ensure that their review processes are conducted mutually with partners.*
> 3. Successful alliances had planning processes that were more similar to the way that their organizations formally planned other aspects of their businesses. *Alliance managers should emulate their*

organizations' formal planning processes for their alliances.[1]

This valuable study suggests that if alliance managers introduce consistent structure to their partnerships, they will increase the chance of realizing success. The authors make these specific recommendations for Partnership and Alliance Managers regarding the planning of alliances:

1. Don't focus exclusively on reviewing actual and projected numbers; ensure that there is sufficient follow through in terms of formal planning approval processes and communication of plans.

2. Work to involve high level executives and stakeholders more in the planning, approval and actual results review processes in order to increase the visibility of major alliances.

3. As much as possible, strive for mutual involvement of both partner organizations in the planning and actual results review processes.

4. Emulate the planning processes already in use throughout the rest of the organization. Even though alliances may be unique in terms of their need to collaborate outside organizational boundaries, by adopting

---

[1] Dave Luvison, Ard-Pieter de Man, Keith Gaylord, *5th State of Alliance Study: Business Planning Processes*, (Canton, Massachusetts, Association of Strategic Alliance Professionals) p. 1.

standard organizational planning processes there is a greater likelihood for organization-wide support and participation.[2]

By having more formalized processes – *structure* – the company's stakeholders are better able to understand the planning process and see how partnerships and alliances fit in the mainstream of their business. The study states: "This offers the advantage of reinforcing the value of the alliance throughout the organization, which in turn can help ensure greater organizational support..."

The referenced study underscores the value of structure as a key ingredient in successful, durable partnerships, as described throughout this book. Some of the recurring themes we will visit that contribute to success:

- ✓ Have clear goals.
- ✓ Document the processes to be followed.
- ✓ Communicate the goals, processes and results frequently and widely.
- ✓ Be inclusive. Share openly with internal stakeholders and counterparties.
- ✓ Mutuality. Having a strong partnership requires treating each partner with respect and being mindful of how each party can be successful as a result of the relationship.

---

[2] Ibid., 12.

4. Outsourcing vs. Partnerships

There is a difference between outsourcing and partnerships. Yes, forming a partnership and having an outsourcing relationship do have certain similarities. But we believe the key difference is that strategic partnerships are designed to deliver value in a more holistic, shared way for the ultimate customer.

The conventional outsourcing arrangement is a more transactional relationship between the outsourcing company and the service provider. Often the interests of the parties are not fully aligned. Whereas in a strategic partnership there is a specific definition of success and the paramount concern is alignment of interests.

Some progressive organizations are moving from transactional outsourcing toward strategic partnerships as a way to get better business results. Author and University of Tennessee professor Kate Vitasek coined the term "Vested Outsourcing" as a progressive outsourcing model that is more collaborative, where everyone wins. The terrific book, **Vested Outsourcing: Five Rules that Will Transform Outsourcing,** describes the scope of this approach and is worth reading by Partnership Managers.

Vitasek describes the vested relationship as follows:

> Vested Outsourcing partnerships create a new relationship category that lies between preferred suppliers and strategic alliances. The relationship is

more focused than the strategic alliance and does not require as much operational infrastructure.[3]

For many years, companies have been outsourcing a variety of business functions to focus on their core areas of expertise. Legendary business consultant Peter Drucker is famous for saying "Do what you do best and outsource the rest."

Today, companies successfully outsource information technology and data center activities, telecommunication, manufacturing, facilities management, financial and accounting processes, human resource functions and many other activities. This is a great way to focus on your core competencies and take advantage of the expertise of other people and organizations to perform specific functions with a high degree of efficiency. Outsourcing functions to a specialist can add value and allow acceleration of production and development for a business. Cognizant, Conduent, Accenture and IBM, for instance, offer a wide range of outsourcing solutions for businesses, including financial services.

---

[3] Kate Vitasek, *Vested Outsourcing – Five Rules That Will Transform Outsourcing*, (New York: Palgrave Macmillan, 2010), p. 41.

5. Impact, Intimacy and Vision

For their book *Getting Partnering Right*, authors Neil Rackham, Lawrence Friedman and Richard Ruff interviewed over a hundred companies to understand what makes partnerships work. They found three common elements in successful partnerships that the authors describe as *impact, intimacy* and *vision*.

> **Impact.** We use the term impact to describe a partnership's capacity to deliver tangible results. Successful partnerships increase productivity, add value, and ultimately, improve profitability. Every successful partnership has impact as its raison d'être.
>
> **Intimacy.** Successful partnerships have moved far beyond transactional relationships and have achieved a level of closeness that would be unrecognizable within the old buyer-seller model. Intimacy is a challenging word; it conjures up images of people relating on an intensely close level. That's exactly what successful partners are doing in a business context.
>
> **Vision.** It is not enough to increase productivity and achieve closeness. Some organizations have both of these elements and yet are not able to make partnerships a reality. Successful partnerships also have vision – a compelling picture of what the part-

nership can achieve and, specifically, how it is going to get there.[4]

The authors do a wonderful job of describing how to advance a possible partnership. Assume you see that there is high impact potential with a relationship. How does the Partnership Manager turn this into a convincing vision? The answer starts by developing a *partnering proposition.* (We call it a *Partnership Goals Statement.*) Essentially, this is a description of what the partnership can achieve for the two organizations and can serve as a platform for further discussion. The *partnering proposition* has the following characteristics:

- It is expressed in terms that are brief, compelling and believable.

- It specifies the impact that each party will gain as a result of the partnership.

- It specifies the major changes that each party must make in order to achieve the impact.

The most successful partnerships are bilateral; there are clear benefits to both sides. And each side is treated with respect. There is genuine concern for mutual success. It is all too common to have discussions about partnerships and lose sight of this critical factor. When one partner treats their counterpart poorly, it will usually turn into an ignominious failure.

---

[4] Neil Rackham, Lawrence Friedman, Richard Ruff, *Getting Partnering Right*, (New York: McGraw-Hill, 1996), pp. 12-13.

To have an effective *partnering proposition,* along with other elements of structure, we suggest giving attention to the value to be derived from a partnership for **both** parties. There should be value for both sides; one side should not feel subordinate to the other.

6. Partnerships Can Lead to Acquisitions

If a strategic partnership is successful, it can lead to a merger or acquisition. While this is usually not the only reason to construct a partnership, it is worth keeping this possibility in mind. And for some, it is the desired endgame.

Many of the steps that go into cultivating a solid partnership and the relationship-building can help pave the road to an acquisition. They also pay significant dividends if an acquisition occurs.

During the partnership, the parties get to know each other and prove the products or services are a good fit. That is, the work that has taken place during the partnership creates value and adds to the reason for an acquisition to take place.

If an ultimate acquisition is desired, the best way to end up with that result is to create business success: close deals, make sales, demonstrate a great working relationship. With success, the chances the other company will want to acquire your business are significantly enhanced. Without success, probably not. So, focus on creating serious value. A partnership can be a great way to test the waters and see if an ultimate acquisition makes sense.

If you desire an acquisition as the outcome and are using partnerships to help get to that point, then structure can help. It is a good idea to ask the partner (potential acquirer) about their criteria for buying other businesses. What is the profile of their acquisition targets? What do they look for in terms of size, growth rate, business area? Knowing this lets you have a direct discussion about a possible acquisition.

For the company seeking to be acquired, establishing strategic partnerships may be a step in that direction. The approach may be:

a. Identify a list of companies that you believe would be well suited to acquire your business.
b. Develop a reason for those companies to buy you. For example, is it filling a product gap? Clearly describe the "white space" your company can fill for the other business. Or is the reason more the ability to add bulk and grow the customer base through a combination?
c. Once these potential suitors are identified, treat them like sales prospects. These are your desired Tier 1 Partners.
d. Identify the right person at the other company. Call on them and ask for a meeting. Explain the value that can be created through a partnership with your business.
e. Continue to follow-up, foster a relationship and build a structured strategic partnership.
f. Measure the results of the partnership.
g. If all goes well, and the desires of both parties are aligned, the partnership may lead to an acquisition transaction.

As mentioned, it is perfectly okay to ask the other company about their appetite for acquisitions and whether the partnership may lead to a transaction. Having a clear understanding about any particular concerns or thoughts that are shared in those discussions can be helpful down the line.

Consider Ikea's acquisition of TaskRabbit, reported in September 2017. The Swedish home goods giant bought the contract labor marketplace company and made the unit an independent subsidiary within Ikea. Previously, the companies had a strategic partnership in place.

The businesses seem complementary. Ikea sells furniture that needs assembly. TaskRabbit offers consumers a platform to deploy people – qualified Taskers – who can do the assembly. After getting to know each other and proving out the fit, Ikea determined it would be best to own TaskRabbit. A leader in the "gig economy" that links freelance workers with jobs, over 50,000 independent workers use the TaskRabbit platform. Here is how the deal was reported by the news site TechCrunch:

> TaskRabbit, the on-demand platform for hiring people to do everything from build furniture to stand in line for you at the Apple Store, has sold itself to IKEA,
>
> TaskRabbit CEO Stacy Brown-Philpot and her staff will remain on board and continue to fulfill their partnerships with other retailers.
>
> "With IKEA Group ownership, TaskRabbit could realize even greater opportunities; increasing the earning potential of Taskers and connecting consumers to a wide range of affordable services," Philpot said in a press release.
>
> This acquisition makes a lot of sense, given that IKEA furniture, in my experience, is hard to put together and can require help from an able-bodied person via TaskRabbit. Last December, IKEA partnered with TaskRabbit to have the on-demand handyperson startup become its official furniture assembler in London.

"In a fast-changing retail environment, we continuously strive to develop new and improved products and services to make our customers' lives a little bit easier," IKEA CEO Jesper Brodin said. "Entering the on-demand, sharing economy enables us to support that. We will be able to learn from TaskRabbit's digital expertise, while also providing IKEA customers additional ways to access flexible and affordable service solutions to meet the needs of today's customer."

7. Partnership Examples

TrueCar

An interesting company that uses partnerships in a major way in their business is TrueCar, Inc.

TrueCar runs a digital automotive marketplace that supplies pricing data about what other people paid for their cars and enables consumers to engage with TrueCar Certified Dealers. TrueCar operates its own branded site for consumers and powers web sites for partners.

These are car-buying programs for some of the largest membership and service organizations, including USAA, AARP, American Express, AAA and Sam's Club.

According to the company, over one third of all new car buyers engage with the TrueCar network during their auto purchasing process.

In August 2016 TrueCar announced a new partnership with J.P. Morgan Chase & Co. to let customers combine shopping for a car and securing of financing for the purchase. The aim is to streamline the process and reduce negotiating at the dealership. Customers start at Chase.com, navigate over to a TrueCar site and then return to the bank's site to submit the loan application and obtain financing in a single session.

Safelite

Another example of a company that has developed a successful partnership strategy is Safelite AutoGlass®. Safelite AutoGlass® fixes more windshields than anyone else in the U.S. It is a member of the Safelite® Group, the world's largest family of retail auto glass companies. The company has been in business since 1947 and employs 12,000 people nationwide.

In addition to replacement services, the company operates a team of repair specialists dedicated to delivering high quality windshield repairs.

Insurance companies, such as Allstate, USAA and Safeco, partner with Safelite to repair damaged windshields for their policyholders.

If a windshield is chipped by a rock or damaged in another way, the policyholder calls their insurance company to report a claim. From that point, Safelite often carries out the window repair or replacement through their partnership with the insurance company.

Costco

When you go to a Costco Wholesale store or visit Costco on-line, you will notice a range of services offered by partners. These services are available to Costco customers (members) through relationships with a number of strategic partners. For example, Payroll Services (QuickBooks), Auto & Home Insurance (Ameriprise), Life Insurance (Protective), Dental Coverage (Delta Dental), Health Insurance.

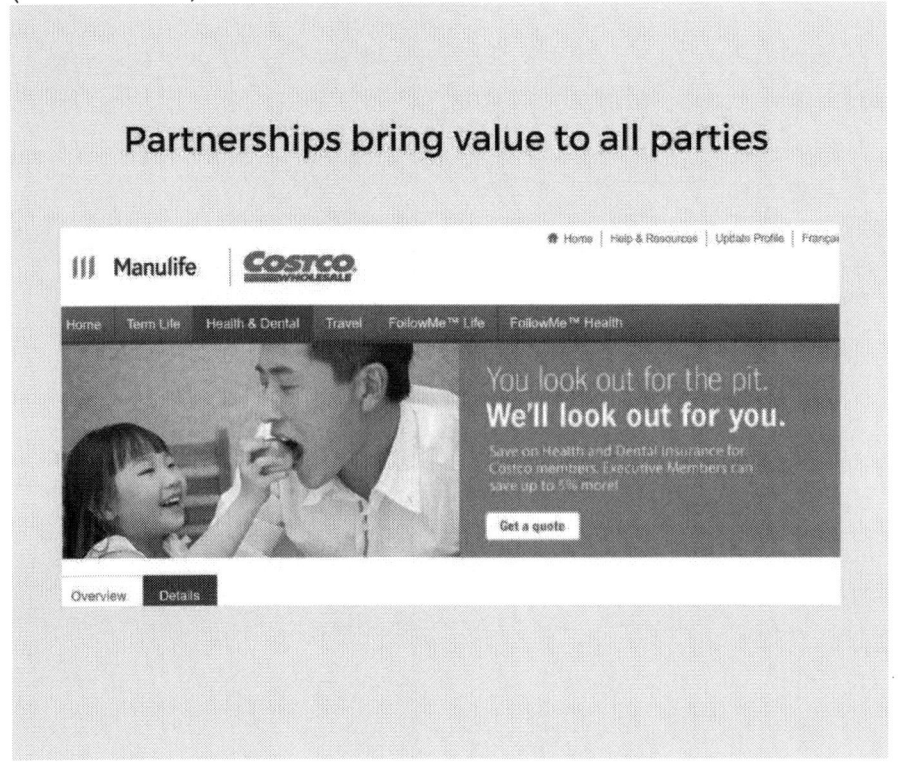

Partnerships bring value to all parties

West Elm

Furniture and home décor retailer West Elm, known for stylish designs at affordable prices and part of Williams–Sonoma, Inc., has developed a partnership with hospitality management and development company DDK to launch West Elm Hotels. The first properties are expected to be in Detroit,

Minneapolis, Savannah, Charlotte and Indianapolis and are planned to begin opening in late 2018.

DDK has over 60 years of combined hospitality and investment experience and has spearheaded the development, launch, and day-to-day management of some of the world's strongest new hospitality brands.

Making the partnership announcement, West Elm leaderships said:

> Together, we're building a first-class management organization to exclusively service the properties in our collection. Our vision is for a truly modern hotel: one that brings together design, technology, and community to create spaces that make everyone feel like they belong. Our top priority is consistent, high-quality service and a locally-driven guest experience.

8. Finding New Partners – Deconstruct Customers

There is a broad range of ways to identify new partners, including researching companies that fit the stated goals for your network. One way that should not be overlooked is by "deconstructing" your current customers.

By deconstructing, we mean to carefully examine your customers and find out:

- What other types of businesses – suppliers, vendors – do your customers work with?

- Who are the other vendors supporting your customers in the type of business where you operate – or adjacent to your area?

Learning about these other vendors and suppliers can be achieved through direct discussions with your contact parties at the customer. Or, your contacts may refer you to others to interview. Ask and they will tell.

Some of the companies identified as a result of this process may be great potential partners for you. That is to say they may closely match the profile you created for quality partner candidates.

Take, for example, a company that is seeking a partner to help enter a specific new territory. By speaking with customers, you may be able to identify other companies which are strong in the region where you are looking to expand.

The review should concentrate on those companies that are in the realm of business where you are focused and meet the other criteria you have established.

Deconstructing customers may point you to some highly qualified prospective partners. Since you already share clients, by definition, you have something in common. And the prospective partners will more than likely be happy to engage with you. If they are not a good fit, they may direct you to another partner who is more suitable.

9. Willing Partners

It may seem obvious that a partnership must have two willing partners to be successful. But we often see situations where one of the partners has certain expectations that are out of line with the other side. This has the ability to impair success. And it will almost certainly cause great stress and friction between the parties.

Having willing partners relates directly to structure. For example, throughout this book we emphasize how standardized procedures are important to track what is going on with existing partnerships. This includes routine reviews of financial results of the partnership, sales and marketing activities, training, technical issues and other elements.

Proven willingness on both sides is a key characteristic that is essential for a successful partnership.

Let's consider a situation where one partner does not share this information. Maybe they are too busy or disorganized to collect the data requested. The companies may still have good reasons to be partners and there may be sales results achieved. Usually, this is an indication that results can actually be much better if more structure was applied.

So how do we solve this problem?

- It is a good idea to introduce the idea of structure before the relationship is set. Make it clear that you believe structure will help foster growth and advance the partnership. Explain the reasons why this is true. For instance, give examples of quarterly checklists to review results and reach agreement on what items will work in this situation. Rather than introducing an unexpected request later on, it is anticipated and becomes a clear part of the relationship.

- Transparency. Make it clear to your partners that the elements included with a structured approach, such as reporting, routine training, financial projections are needed for your internal obligations. Everyone has a boss and Partnership Managers have to demonstrate activity and results. The cooperation and support of partner companies is necessary to carry out those commitments.

- Communication. Explaining – sometimes repeatedly – that structure and the associated elements are needed is a part of the job of a Partnership Manager and Alliance Specialist.

- Emphasize the need for data. Businesses need data to track progress and succeed. When a partner is not willing to provide data or collaborate on how the data will be gathered and presented, try explaining that the information is necessary to manage the partnership and the business as a whole. Sometimes highlighting that data drives success puts the need for structure in a better context for some people.

If a long block of time passes between reviewing a partnership and discussing how to enhance the relationship, it is never a good thing. Structure is meant to be a way for partners to stay in tune with each other's needs and to plan accordingly.

The **willingness and cooperation** of both parties is always needed for a partnership to succeed and make a positive difference for all. Even the most logical partnership with the greatest potential won't work without a high level of willingness on both sides.

10. Alignment and Balance Are Critical for Success

A lot of time can be wasted on partners who are fishing around for you to sell their products. These fishermen call or e-mail and state they have a great product or service and want partners just like you. In fact, they have done little research on your product or service. Often, there may not even be a logical linkage and value proposition for clients. And usually they have nothing real to offer. They are trying to gain access to your resources: sales, expertise, marketing, customers. It takes so little work on their part. Shutting the fishermen down and sending them packing is a key responsibility for Partnership Managers. Resources are scarce and they cannot be wasted by entertaining non-strategic partnerships that offer little chance of delivering success.

Of importance to all Partnership Managers is making sure the companies they are partnering with are a strategic match. Without a common strategic outlook and plan for the future, it is hard to move forward. If the strategic match is not present, it is usually not a good idea to proceed with the partnership. There is no amount of structure that can make it work.

In his article "Creating Effective Partnerships," Dave Brock with the consulting firm Partners in Excellence, based in Mission Viejo, California, says effective partnerships are a combination of the following factors:

> **Shared Risk:** Each partner bears a fair and appropriate share of the risk in the alliance. No partner has a disproportionate level of risk.

Shared Resources: Each partner commits an appropriate proportion of the resources, whether they are capital, people, knowledge, technology or other.

Shared Rewards: Each partner shares appropriately in the rewards, the partners work together to create mutual wins.

Shared Vision: The partners share a common view of the objectives, results and outcomes of the alliance. They share a common vision of the importance of the relationship.

Shared Values: They share common value systems and complementary cultures. This shared value system is the bedrock of the relationship, providing the means, motivation and commitment to resolve problems with the relationship and growing the relationship.

Without each of these elements, the partnership is unbalanced and unaligned. The more unbalanced the relationship, the higher the likelihood that the partnership will fail to achieve its objectives. We all know that if all the risk is borne by one partner, that partner will feel they are being taken advantage of. Lack of alignment in the relationship sows the seeds of distrust driving the alliance into a death spiral.[5]

---

[5] Dave Brock, *Creating Effective Strategic Partnerships, (Mission Viejo, CA, 2003)*

11. The Structured Partnership Framework

We have broken down the strategic partnership process into three categories: *Choosing, Roll-Out and Managing*.

Of course, this does not cover every aspect of establishing and growing partnerships. But it is our hope we can address enough components to bring something to the table for everyone involved with designing and expanding businesses through these arrangements. Structure adds confidence, brings consistency and helps ensure great outcomes.

In *Mastering Alliance Strategy*, the authors state that "Companies operating successful alliances tend to have a definite approach to how they develop alliance strategies, select partners, structure the deal, and plan for evolution." Companies need to understand these seven common alliance pitfalls:

- Unclear objectives
- Lack of a detailed business plan;
- Decision gridlock;
- Aligning with a weak or competitive partner;
- Unmanaged cultural clash;
- Failure to learn or protect core capabilities;
- Failure to plan for alliance evolution. [6]

We will look at how structure can help avoid these pitfalls and lead to strong results for your partnerships.

---

[6] James D. Bamford, Benjamin Gomes-Casseres, Michael Robinson, *Mastering Alliance Strategy: A Comprehensive Guide to Design, Management and Organization*, (San Francisco: John Wiley & Sons Inc., 2003), p. 24.

Looking at key elements within these three phases - *Choosing, Roll-Out and Managing* - we come up with the following framework:

The Structured Partnership Framework

Choosing Partners
- Develop a Partnership Goals Statement - Address financial, strategic, marketing and product goals. Create a one-page statement of what is to be achieved through partnerships. This can be shared with internal business leaders and partners or potential partners.
- Identify prospective partners with proven willingness.
- Have partners complete the Initial Partner Review questionnaire.
- Evaluate Fit: chemistry, culture, shared vision, goals.
- Put the partner agreement in place and set specific, measurable goals to be achieved.

Roll-Out of New Partnerships *(The Launch)*
- Identify all stakeholders involved to implement the partnership and make it a success. *Include internal managers and business unit leaders.*
- Prepare and reach agreement on the Partner Roll-Out Plan. Make it a living document.
- Summarize the financial terms and billing arrangement.
- Put the partnership agreement in place.
- Make sure there is willingness to do the work – all parties
- Communicate. Build excitement "buzz" about the partnership.

Managing
- Create a Clear Business Plan
- Monitor activity

- Ongoing training of the relevant stakeholders: sales, account management, etc.
- Try to get an early win
- Quarterly Business Reviews.
- Annual Partner Reviews, Audits or Health Checks.

12. State Your Goals

As with so many business processes, the first step is to clearly state your goals. Organize your thoughts and write them down. It is imperative to concisely state your main goals – in essence a summary of your strategy - for having partnerships. A one-page *Partnership Goals Statement* will usually do the trick.

In the publication from PwC's Deal's Practice titled *Joint Ventures and Strategic Alliances*, the authors note:

> Put strategy first. Start with a strategy not a partner. A well-understood strategy underpins the path to a successful alliance. Strategy will also determine the optimal alliance partner. A sound strategy provides a framework and foundation for executing growth objectives.[7]

This *Partnership Goals Statement* can be used in a variety of messages and communications. It can be shared with prospective partners and internal managers.

For example, the *Partnership Goals Statement* might list one or more items that are a company's focus, such as:

- Generate more revenue by having a strategic partner to sell our products or services to their customers in the automotive sector.

---

[7] Greg McGahan, Nigel Smith, Curt Moldenhauer, *Joint Ventures and Strategic Alliances – Examining the keys to success, (PricewaterhouseCoopers, LLC, 2016), p. 15.*

- Enter a new target market segment or geography by developing a relationship with a partner already established in that market. Identified markets are heavily regulated industries such as finance and utilities.

- Forge a partnership with a company that will give us access to a product or service desired by our customers and fits with the value proposition we deliver in the market.

- Bring a new, innovative offering to the market by combining our product or service with another complementary solution.

- Improve customer loyalty by having a broader set of products or services available. Enhance the value chain offered in the market.

- Cost savings. Allow us to concentrate on our strongest core offerings and work with a partner for certain aspects of our product set.

13. Profile of the Possible Partner

Once the high-level goals are stated, the next step is to identify the profile of the partner. Write it down. We find it useful to have the established profile ready to reveal to potential partners and internal managers.

Include a set of candid points describing in blunt terms what it would take to meet the goals you identified. Below are a few examples:

- Shared Values. If the values of the partner are not aligned with yours, there is no level of structure that will make it a success. Describe your core values and approach to business. See if that matches with the values of the possible partner company.

- The partner sought offers a service sold to firms in the *(leisure and hospitality, semiconductor...)* sector.

- The partner sought has an incumbent customer base in the *(leisure and hospitality, semiconductor...)* market with over 500 active clients.

- The partners have an ability to introduce, sell and understand each other's products/solutions. *(Sometimes, one company is completely focused on a particular product that is sold to a defined customer and the economic buyer is in a specific role. It can be difficult to introduce another product that is outside of that area.)*

- The buyer of the partner's product or service is the (*Vice President of Supply Chain Management or Procurement or Finance.*)

- The partner sought will have an established sales force and account management team working with clients and prospects in the target market.

- The partner and your company have complementary capabilities. This can include products, technology, target market, size and profile of customer base, geography served.

- The partner is not a competitor. Having a competitor as a partner introduces a high risk of conflict and diminishes the chance of success.

- The partner is able to commit the necessary resources – people, time, money – to build the relationship over time.

- The partner agrees to the structured approach to manage and monitor the relationship.

- The partner understands the strategic purpose you are seeking to accomplish and all parties believe the relationship can support that stated strategy.

- Trust. Only work with people you trust. There is an untold amount of risk otherwise. And life is way too short.

14. Presenting Structure to Partners

As the Partnership Manager, you may care to present a summary of the structure approach to your new or existing partners. This will give them a clear sense of what to expect when working with you. In many cases, they have not encountered this approach before. So, it is only fair to lay out the framework and have a discussion about how the approach is designed to have partnerships that are strong and resilient.

We like to think that structure adds organization and credibility to any Strategic Partnership program. Using partnerships, as we know, is an effective way to grow revenue, expand the business, reach new markets and fill product gaps. And the setting is right for the use of partnerships across many different market sectors. It becomes critical to position yourself as a *Partner of Choice*.

What goes into being a *Partner of Choice* is the responsibility of the Partnership Manager. When those elements are defined, they can be communicated to the market. This includes sharing the description with existing and prospective partners and internal managers. The questions to be answered include:

- ✓ What differentiates your partnership program from others?
- ✓ Why should a partner select to do business with you?
- ✓ From the partner's point of view, what are the advantages of working together?

For example, in your quest to be a ***Partner of Choice*** you might share with the partner, or prospect, a trenchant outline showing the elements that will help in fostering a successful partnership and are expected as part of the relationship:

1. A *Partner Agreement*
2. Having a *Business Plan* for the partnership
3. Putting a *Partner Roll Out Plan* in place
4. Sales projections agreed to by the parties
5. Training commitments
6. Quarterly and annual meetings to review the status of the partnership.

For many companies, it is a good idea to promote their partnership program to prospects. Explain to the market how your partnership program is constructed and why partnering with you is desirable and can create value. A convenient way to do this is by including on the company's website an overview of the program and a way for prospective partners to submit inquiries.

15. Presenting Structure to Your Internal Team

We looked at communicating your approach to partnerships to both current and prospective partners. It is also a good idea to share information about your methods with internal managers. This may include business unit leaders, corporate executives and other managers.

One way to do this is to have a simple, periodic e-mail update shared with the group summarizing your activities, successes, goals and encouraging feedback from colleagues.

To be effective, the message should be built around a strong central theme, such as supporting company growth. Keep your partnerships in the context of the overall company's goals and mission.

An added benefit of this communication is that it can spur interest and buy-in regarding partnerships and even stimulate ideas about quality organizations to consider as potential partners.

At a time when everyone is bombarded with content and e-mails, keeping it brief is critical. Give your team a sense of what is going on in the partnership area; track the partners you have in place and what you are looking to accomplish.

Of course, we suggest including something about the structured approach to give managers a genuine understanding of what is expected of current and future partners.

Internal communication can contribute to your success and help prevent partnerships from going off the rails.

How to Succeed with Internal Stakeholders

Communicating with your internal stakeholders at the different stages of partnerships is also a good idea.

New Partnerships: Give your internal colleagues early notice about a potential new partnership that is under consideration. Try to gather their views about the planned relationship and how it might impact their area of responsibility.

Roll Out: Let stakeholders know the launch schedule and get consent that the timing works for everyone.

Ongoing Management Updates: Keep your team advised about progress being made with existing partnerships will add to the support and harmony you have with all stakeholders. As mentioned, a routine, brief internal update can be effective for keeping everyone clued in about your activities.

Choosing Partners

16. How to Choose the Right Partner

One of the main reasons for writing this book is to suggest a clear process for identifying and selecting new partners. This includes defining what you are looking for and a structured way to screen potential partners.

Choosing the right partner is a strong factor in the results achieved. In equal measure, factors to consider include:

- The strategic fit between the companies;
- How complementary are the strengths and practices of each partner;
- Cultures of the partners;
- Degree of commitment to the relationship;
- Chemistry between the managers at both companies.

In *Cases in Alliance Management*, co-authors and Management Professors, Jean-Louis Schaan, Ph.D. and Micheál J. Kelly, Ph.D, write:

> It invariably takes longer than anticipated to find the right partner. Regardless of whether a company proactively searches for a partner based on its identified needs or it is approached by another company, it is important to commit the time and resources to thoroughly analyze the potential opportunity. Depending on the scope and complexity of the alliance, it may take several months or even years to complete the deal.

Furthermore, in many cases, there is likely to be more than one right partner. Hence, it is important to invest the time to determine which potential partner is best positioned to meet a company's strategic needs. Small companies looking for alliance partners are often tempted to look for shortcuts as they find themselves facing time and financial pressures. They may succumb to the temptation to partner with any company that expresses a willingness to partner, whether or not it meets their strategic needs. Invariably, this move is a mistake.[8]

Even before assigning names to the list of potential partners, the Partner Manager should develop a profile of what the right partner looks like. Jean-Louis Schaan and Micheál J. Kelly recommend using the following matrix to help create a profile of the ideal partner - before identifying specific companies:

List **partner competencies** sought. (e.g., Customer base, IP, infrastructure, etc.)	#1
	#2
What are the characteristics of a partner that would find **our core competencies** desirable?	#1
	#2
What is the **ideal size and structure** of a partner?	#1
	#2

---

[8] Jean-Louis Schaan and Micheál J. Kelly, *Cases in Alliance Management: Building Successful Alliances*, (Thousand Oaks: Sage Publications, Inc. 2007), pp. 93-95.

What are some **key relationships** we would like the partner to bring to the table? (e.g., Tier 1 customers, suppliers)	#1 #2
What other factors are of crucial importance to our partner selection? (e.g., track record)	#1 #2

It is critical for the Partnership Manager at a company to quickly and easily let potential partners know what you are seeking to achieve and what you require in terms of a partnership. Letting potential partners know about your structured approach and that everyone is expected to follow it can lead to constructive, quality conversations. This alone may send some potential partners packing. That's okay. They are not the ones you want to do business with anyway.

The basic steps a Strategic Partnership Manager uses in identifying potential partners can be summarized as:

Four Basic Steps to Identify Strategic Partners

1. Develop the criteria for the partnership – a specific checklist of characteristics and capabilities.
2. Identify potential partners that seem to meet the criteria you have established.

3. Short List the potential candidates. Come up with the top three candidates and focus on those companies to see if a partnership can be developed.
4. Conduct discussions and due diligence.

17. Sample Initial Partner Questionnaire

When considering a new partner, we find it valuable to have readily available a set of questions for the prospective partner to complete. This is useful whether the prospective partner has initiated the discussion or if you have started the dialogue and are pursuing this company.

There are several benefits associated with this approach of having a brief set of questions to present:

- Clarify the goals of a partnership;
- Gain an understanding of the other company or person seeking to be your partner;
- Produce a framework for further discussions.

As we know, there are many people in partnership roles that call or e-mail companies (you may receive these) to say:

"How about we have a partnership? My product or service is awesome and you will be doing your clients a great favor by letting them know about it. When do you want to start making money?"

What happens next? The Partnership Manager wants to hear about possible opportunities and find new ways that can help clients and grow the company. A likely next step is to listen and learn more about the inquiring company and their products.

This early discussion is critical to set the proper course. The Initial Business Review shown at the end of this chapter is an example of what might be sent to a prospective partner ("Lincoln" in this illustration) early in the discussions about a possible relationship. Of course, the specific questions would be modified based on the type of business.

It is recommended to keep this brief and simple to complete. The goal is to gather some baseline information and create an understanding of the business, not to conduct due diligence. This is provided after the parties put in place a Confidentiality Agreement or Non-Disclosure Agreement (NDA.) Appendix 3 of this book includes a sample Mutual Confidentiality Agreement.

At this stage, you are trying to get an assessment of the business, the market they serve and their thoughts about a partnership. While it is a short homework assignment, some will not put forth the effort to respond. If the potential partner takes a long time to fulfill the request or does not respond, it is a good indication of how they think and operate.

From: Strategic Partnership Manager

To: Lincoln (Potential Partner)

Re: Initial Business Review

In connection with a review of Lincoln as a potential strategic partner, below are questions to help us understand more about your business and products and help guide our future discussions. Please complete and return with your responses.

1. Review of Lincoln's primary products, services and value supplied to clients. How do the core products/services benefit customers?
   a. Product A
   b. Product B
2. Describe the main market segment you sell to. Why is this segment of the market your focus?
3. Supply a brief profile of your target customer.
4. Describe the technology used at Lincoln.
5. Organization. Supply a description of staff and management. Discuss the current roles and what is needed going forward.
   a. Operations
   b. Sales and Marketing
   c. Finance
   d. Technology
   e. Client Services/Account Management
6. Describe your sales process.
7. Volume analysis. Provide a review of business volume, by product or service offering for the last two years and this year. Is the company growing? At what rate?
8. Do you see the potential partnership as mutual? That is, we will sell/introduce your products/service to our cus-

tomers and you will sell/introduce our products/services to your customers?
9. Describe other strategic partnerships you have now, or had in the recent past. How have they worked out?

18. Sales Projections Are Necessary from the Start

There is often uncertainty about the level of revenue to be generated from a new partnership. There is always a ramp-up period and it is not easy to predict with accuracy what will be accomplished. To be sure, it takes time to implement and build a partnership. But in business it is also necessary to establish real goals and monitor performance. In fact, with a structured approach to partnerships it is imperative to set goals and this includes sales projections.

The thought of preparing sales projections for new partnerships makes some managers cheer while others wince. It is easy to say: *Let's give it some time and see what the response is in the market.* That approach is a mistake. It is better to put a stake in the ground, use sound judgment, best efforts, make smart assumptions and produce projections early on.

Sales projections are needed to measure progress and establish a framework for what is expected from a partnership. Both sides of the partnership should have these projections. Ideally, they are developed in collaboration. But even if one partner prepares the projections, they should be shared with both sides and discussed.

Having sales projections and communicating them will lead to managers taking the partnership more seriously. What's more, it recognizes the reality that revenue and revenue growth is the mainstay of any business.

What is the best method for coming up with goals, especially with a new partnership where there is not much of a track record to use as a guide?

A best practice is for the Partnership Manager to collaborate with the sales leaders of both companies. Get a sense of prior experience with the roll-out of other products or partnerships. How long did it take to make actual sales and what was the penetration rate? Consider the number of clients in the company. A model can be built to sell to a portion of that base. For example, 1% penetration in year 1 and 2% in year 2. These projections will give the partnership manager credibility with business leaders. How ambitious you make the goals is dependent on the good business sense of the Partnership Manager, sales leaders and product experts.

Even with limited data, assumptions can be made and a sales projection for year one and year two can be developed. For example:

Year 1 2021	1st Qtr.	2nd Qtr.	3rd Qtr.	4th Qtr.	Total
Number of Sales	5	8	10	15	38
Revenue	$ 50,000	$ 80,000	$ 100,000	$ 250,000	$480,000

Year 2 2022	1st Qtr.	2nd Qtr.	3rd Qtr.	4th Qtr.	Total
Number of Sales	20	24	26	28	98
Revenue	$ 200,000	$ 240,000	$ 260,000	$ 280,000	$980,000

19. Prioritize and Focus

As mentioned earlier, a challenge in identifying, developing and managing partnerships is getting caught up with certain partners who may not be the ones that can contribute the most toward your goals. Resist the temptation to spend too much time and resources on partners or potential partners who just don't fit or have little strategic value to offer. The cost of spending time with these is that the great partners (or the best potential partners) are ignored. This sounds basic but it is often the difference between an enormously successful partnership program and one that is flat.

The solution is to identify the best partners, or potential partners, and have the discipline to focus efforts there. Alternatively, we spend a lot of time on less important partners and never get to the ones that can deliver the greatest results. Marketing Strategist Al Ries wrote about narrowing the scope of one's business to be successful and standing for something in the minds of customers and the market. In his book *Focus: The Future of Your Company Depends On It*, Ries writes: "A focus implies a "narrowing" of the business with the intent to dominate a segment. There's power when you can "own" a market. There's no power when you are a bit player."[9]

Prioritize partners and potential partners. Consider creating three tiers:

Tier 1 – Top partners. This segment of partners should receive the most attention and resources. Weekly calls or

---
[9] Al Ries, *Focus: The Future of Your Company Depends On It* (New York: HarperBusiness, 1996), p. 289.

meetings. Quarterly business reviews. A written Business Plan is in place laying out the established goals and steps to be accomplished. The most time is spent here. A variety of initiatives are happening, including cross-training of the teams on the relevant products. Other activities are created and there is strong commitment from both sides to achieve results. Metrics are established and agreed upon for how success will be measured.

Tier 2 – Strategic partnerships that have been determined to be a good fit with your goals and the companies are committed to maintaining and growing the relationship. Routine contact with the stakeholders, training sessions, product reviews, marketing activities and sales initiatives are underway.

Tier 3 – These are partnerships that are good to have in place but get less attention and resources. The fit is established. There are agreed upon activities and an established commitment from the parties in regard to sales, marketing, product development and other relevant areas. There is potential here but these partnerships are "average" and there cannot be much time dedicated to them.

Depending on your situation and resources, it may be a good idea to confine your attention to Tier 1 partners.

Devoting all of your time and energy on the best possibilities will increase your chance of success. There is a lot to be said for focus. Usually, focus leads to greater results by eliminating distractions and less promising opportunities.

20. Proactively Reach Out to the Best Prospects

Tier 1 partners may already be in place at your company. These are the best partners. Those that offer a great fit with your strategic goals and have a shared chemistry.

If the Tier 1 partners are not already in place, they may be on your prospect list - wish list. It is important that the Partnership Manager is proactively reaching out to the appropriate contacts at the Tier 1 partners. These have been identified as having the greatest potential for future growth and success.

Too often, we allow ourselves to get busy with Tier 2 or 3 partners and have no time left over to spend on the ones that really count the most: Tier 1.

What's more, you may consider the companies in Tier 1 to be the optimal partners but *they* may still need time and convincing to come to that realization. That requires effort.

The following are a few suggestions to help focus on potential Tier 1 partnerships that you <u>do not</u> already have in place:

- ✓ Identify the top three partners for your company. Those are your Tier 1 prospects. Work fervently to engage with them and demonstrate the value of working together.

- ✓ Put together a **Strategic Partner Plan** for each of them. It might include: identifying the strategic Partnership Manager at that company, thoroughly researching the partner, writing the business case as to why the partnership should exist, how the partnership will benefit both parties and customers.

✓ Dedicate a set amount of time each week to spend on cultivating the relationship with those Tier 1 companies. Put it on your calendar.

Engaging with the best prospects on a regular basis will help contribute to ultimate success. It may take time to put the relationship together as desired. Usually, persistence pays off.

21. The Business Case for a Partnership

Some companies put in place a process where they develop a business case for a potential partnership during the formation stage. The business case may be reviewed and approved internally before proceeding with a partnership, or it may be used as a way for the Partnership Manager to organize data and prioritize opportunities.

In the excellent book, **Strategic Alliances: Three Ways to Make Them Work**, author Steve Steinhilber, discusses his experiences with partnerships and alliances at tech giant Cisco.

> Before everyone sits down and negotiates the deal, it's vital to set the stage for a collaborative relationship. Cisco uses what we call a 'shared strategic map' to flesh out, in explicit detail, what the potential partnership will entail so that the parties can learn whether a relationship is mutually beneficial and, if it is, how a potential alliance would operate. Your map should answer such big-picture questions as:
>
> - What is the vision, strategy, and mission of the alliance?
> - What is the value proposition for the customer?
> - What factors are drawing the companies together?
> - What are the opportunities for collaboration and what are the potential liabilities?

- Are the two companies' goals aligned? Can their organizations work together effectively?
- What is a possible joint solution? How could it be deployed to the customer?
- Have the companies targeted a specific customer base?
- What is the delivery, service, and support strategy for the joint offering?
- What will constitute success, and how will it be measured? What are the milestones in the relationship?

The key deliverable at this stage is a joint business plan that outlines the opportunity, the assets each company will bring to the relationship, and the investment model that will establish the foundation for the relationship.

The creation of a shared strategic map uncovers the strengths and weaknesses of a potential partnership and makes it apparent whether the two organizations should move forward. A positive answer should solidify and even quantify the case for a partnership – and serve as a springboard as the alliance moves into action.[10]

Using the business case approach is a terrific practice. It helps in the evaluation of potential partnerships and forces associates to think through and answer the critical questions. The

---

[10] Steve Steinhilber, *Strategic Alliances: Three Ways to Make Them Work (Boston: Harvard Business Press, 2008), pp. 25-27.*

business case serves as a thorough assessment of the potential partnership and helps the company decide if they should consummate the deal.

Following is a sample Partnership Business Case template to consider.

Sample Business Case Template

---

1. **Executive Summary**

   - Background/Current State - What is the business situation that led to this case being written?
   - Desired State - What is this business proposition going to accomplish? Include market opportunity, strategic fit, and revenue, cost and/or margin projections.
   - Recommendation - What decisions are expected from executives regarding this case?

2. **Strategic Assessment**

   - Strategic Fit – Describe why it makes sense for Company to engage in this business. For example: complementary offerings, channel extension, alignment with current initiatives, filling a gap, customer needs.
   - Market Attractiveness – Define "the market" for the business and discuss the size and complexity of the opportunity (impact of the number of players). Include in your discussion

information regarding the anticipated share Company can hope to attain and the timing to do so.
- Competitive Analysis – Who are the competitors and what are their positions in the market? Discuss this proposal's advantages and/or disadvantages relative to the competition. Is there anything unique about this competitive landscape that should be noted?
- Deal Structure – Identify the partnership type and define the proposed contract terms. Identify which party will ultimately contract with the customer. What are the assumed service level agreements between Company and the partner?
- Internal Strengths - What strengths does Company have that will help build or maintain a competitive advantage?
- Internal Weaknesses - In which areas does Company have a weakness that can impede the success of the business?
- External Opportunities - Is there anything happening politically, socially, economically, or technologically that will create future opportunities for this business?
- External Threats - List political (example: change in government regulations), social, economic (change in business cycles – inflation, recession), or technological (obsolescence, substitutes) factors that could threaten the success of this business in the future
- Critical Success Factors – list any factors that you believe will be critical to the success of this business (e.g. development integration, marketing or capital investment, check-the-box sales dependency, timeliness of execution)

3. **Financial Assessment**
- Revenue - Discussion of applicable recurring and non-recurring revenues, book-to-bill timing, pricing, unit forecast.
- Expense - Discussion of capitalized and non-capitalized expenses, labor requirements within each department.

- Finance Operations - Identify who will be responsible for Finance related matters, which party bills the customer and financial metrics that will have to be put in place? Will this business cause change in any Finance/Accounting processes? If so, what are the changes and the labor cost impact?
- Pro Forma P&L - Attach a 3-year forecast with assumptions.
- What risk(s) can be identified?

4. **Sales Assessment**
   - Go to market Strategy (by segment, if it differs by segment)
   - Describe how the product will be marketed and sold – value proposition, etc.
   - Describe rules of engagement.
   - Identify specific sales groups eligible to sell the product(s).
   - Will new sales resources be required?
   - What risk(s) can be identified?

5. **HR / Learning and Development**
   - Sales Training Strategy – what resources are required for sales training and what should the curriculum include? What is the required time commitment for training? Internal and External
   - What risk(s) can be identified?
   - What are critical success factors in this area?

6. **Implementation Assessment**
   - Implementation Strategy (if applicable) - discuss how the business will be implemented, once sold (not rolled out to the market). Be sure to include potential labor hours, and any process changes or creations that are required.
   - What risk(s) can be identified?

- What are critical success factors in this area?

7. **Service and Operations Assessment**
   - Service and Operations Strategy – discuss the service model that will be used for this partnership. If Company is providing tier one service to the customer, what current processes need to be adapted in order to deliver this service?
   - What will be the impact on labor hours? How will this service model impact Company's ability to deliver its service?
   - What operational processes need to be changed to accommodate this business?
   - What risk(s) can be identified?

8. **Product Assessment**
   - Product Strategy – define the products to be offered, its features, and target customers.
   - How does the product interface/integrate with Company's products or services?
   - How does it fit in the roadmap?
   - Describe, in general, the required development work. Be sure to include the required effort (estimate of labor hours) and timing.
   - What risks can be identified?

9. **Technology Assessment**
   - Describe the technology strategy and points of integration from an IT perspective.
   - What is the scope of the requirements and high-level IT development effort to meet those requirements?
   - Describe the IT architecture of the company.
   - Describe any compatibility issues with Company's current infrastructure.

- What APIs are to be used?
- What will it take to bring about the necessary level of compatibility? Be sure to include required labor, software, and hardware.
- What risks can be identified?
- What are critical success factors in this area?

10. **Marketing Assessment**
    - Marketing Strategy - Given the business proposal, describe the marketing approach.
    - Identify the resource requirements to support the proposed revenue targets.
    - What risks can be identified?
    - What are critical success factors in this area?

11. **Partner Assessment** – *Discuss Company's impact to the partner's current business in relation to:*
    - Significance of Company's business to the partner – Will Company become its largest or a major partner, or one of several like players? What is Company's revenue impact to the partner?
    - Partner's market position – How can Company's partnership support the partner's current market position?
    - Statement of Partner's Commitment – Evaluate the partner's concurrence and commitment of revenue and service assumptions
    - What risks might Company experience from the partner's performance?

12. **Risk Assessments** – *List all risks discussed in the above sections. If related, attempt to combine them to support a single idea. Be sure to include the following:*

- Financial Risks – Revenue forecast probabilities including pricing and discounting, expense forecast including partner payments (i.e. royalties, revenue share),
- Legal Risks – Regulatory compliance, intellectual property
- Technology Risks – Obsolescence, incompatibility
- Market risks – Market reaction, or market impact for failure to pursue this partnership.

22. Reseller Arrangements

Sometimes the Partnership Manager may find that a reseller arrangement may be the most suitable type of relationship among the parties. While some do not feel there is a great difference between a partnership or alliance and a reseller structure, we consider the reseller arrangement synonymous with "white-label" or OEM (original equipment manufacturers.) An OEM is a company that makes a part or subsystem that is used in another company's end product. If Russell Manufacturing Co. makes parts that are used in Dell computers, Russell is an OEM.

For this discussion, we will consider a reseller arrangement when one party owns a product and the other party takes it and makes it their own. They might make it part of their own product or solution and often use their identifiable brand and design. And they go on to sell the product as their own. The original owner is invisible to the ultimate customer. Generally speaking, those customers identify the product with the reseller and turn to the reseller after the sales cycle for support and service.

As the Partnership Manager you may find it advantageous to clearly state that you are open to - or even prefer - resellers for a certain product or service. This is the situation we encountered with a software solution called STAYview. The technology solution was developed by HRsoft to implement and manage stay interviews. It is a Cloud-based software product that is used by employers to facilitate a discussion between managers and associates who work for those managers. The goal is to improve employee engagement and retention by having direct conversations and follow-up about what the manager can do for the associates on their team. This software manages the scheduling of conversations (stay interviews), tracks the information identified during the discussions and aggregates data to produce meaningful reports.

We recognized that the software is well-suited to combine with human resource consulting services offered by a variety of firms specializing in this area. The consultants would help the employer introduce the program, train mangers, review the data collected and make recommendations to their client on operational and other business changes. Software could be part of a broader engagement which includes consulting services and the technology.

With this broader engagement approach in mind, we reached out to human resource advisory and consulting firms with the idea that they could be a reseller of our STAYview software. The consultant would combine it with their services and bring value to clients. We committed to host the software, provide training for the consultants and ongoing technical support, including product enhancements to continue to refine the software offering. To clearly describe what we had in mind a brief document was produced and shared with interested parties. Excerpts of that document are shown on the following pages.

HRsoft STAYview Consulting Partner Program

Introduction

This is an overview of the HRsoft STAYview Consulting Partner Program.

HRsoft has created this program to expand distribution of the STAYview software solution and add value to the client experience.

Importantly, the STAYview Partner Program allows HRsoft's Consulting Partners to build a book of recurring software revenue and create additional opportunities to generate consulting revenue.

The STAYview Partner Program was established to increase distribution of valuable STAYview software through HR consulting firms. Ideal partners have expertise and practices focused on improving retention and employee engagement.

Partner Program Details

HRsoft seeks to develop an ongoing business relationship with interested firms who possess these characteristics:

a. An existing human resource or talent management consulting practice in place.
b. Offers other services or products that are a strong fit with Stay Interviews.
c. Employee engagement and retention expertise.
d. Other complementary offerings where STAYview can be a part of the broader engagement with a client.
e. Customer-centric attitude in relationship with clients.

f. Excellent communication skills. Ability to present critical information to high level executives and business leaders.
g. Ability to solve problems.
h. Will represent HRsoft well in the market, since there is a direct connection between the Partner and our brand.

Under the program, the Consulting Partner:

- Sells subscriptions to the STAYview software as an effective tool to help clients improve employee retention and engagement.

- Generates additional consulting assignments for their firm as a result of training the clients' managers and supervisors on the proper way to conduct Stay Interviews and related items, such as taking action based on results of interviews.

- Have new opportunities for periodic check-ins with clients to evaluate employee retention and engagement trends and suggest additional strategies to create improvement.

Benefits for Partners

Over time, the consulting firm can accumulate a book of recurring annual or monthly revenue from selling the product.

The consultant maintains the client relationships, contracts with and bills the client directly for training, consulting and other professional services. HRsoft's interaction with the client is focused on the software implementation and routine technical support as required.

Rolling Out New Partnerships

23. Roll-Out – Introducing New Partnerships

The new partnership deal is signed and the parties are excited to start working together. All of the ideas discussed are ready to be put into a plan of action.

In this section we will look at ways to bring structure to the Roll-Out phase. The amount of time needed for rolling out a new partnership will, of course, vary depending on the complexity involved, availability of people and resources and other factors. To put this in perspective, let's assume that the roll-out of a new partnership will take four months as we consider how we will achieve the identified components.

A recommendation is to set a realistic go-live date and dates for achieving established milestones along the way. Include those dates in the *Roll-Out Plan*. This is a document, spreadsheet, or on-line project plan the Partnership Manager creates and manages throughout the process. Sure, the dates can move. But without real dates, things are much more likely to slip and accountability becomes amorphous.

Like in many relationships, the early days are critical to having a successful, lasting partnership. Structure at the roll-out phase is critical. Essentially, this is the time to put in place a Roll-Out Plan to address what has to happen, who is going to do those things and when they will be done.

What we are referring to as a *Roll-Out Plan*, some people call their Checklist, Punch List, Flight Plan or Project Plan.

Since internal constituents at your company are critical to the success of a partnership, it is important to address internal collaboration as part of the Roll-Out plan. Make the Roll-Out Plan as inclusive as you can. In regard to internal leaders and resources, consider:

- ✓ What do internal colleagues need to know?
- ✓ Who has the needed capabilities?
- ✓ What hurdles might exist?
- ✓ What is a realistic schedule to follow?

It is recommended to state the goals for the roll-out and briefly restate the goals of the partnership in this document. The goals of the roll-out period might include:

- Establish targets for sales;
- Accomplish awareness of the partnership among internal sales, account management and other relevant leaders and teams;
- Conduct training sessions for internal teams;
- Complete initial marketing activities:
  - News Release,
  - Collateral;
  - Announcements to clients;
- Develop the IT integration approach.

The Roll-Out Plan can be extremely detailed or kept at a higher level. There is a case to be made for either approach. A high-level plan can allow the team to focus on certain core areas and not feel overly-burdened. On the other hand, the detailed plan leaves less to chance or misunderstanding.

A granular plan can be suitable in some situations while a high-level plan is sufficient in others. We will look at both. But some form of a written plan is necessary for every partnership to establish the key steps for success.

We cannot emphasize enough the importance of this plan.

We have seen too many situations where research is completed, a proof-of-concept is done and a great partnership is developed. Then it is not rolled out properly – in a structured manner. Of course, this leads to poor results, a less than stellar partnership and creates disappointment throughout both organizations. Eventually, the partnership falls by the wayside and the opportunity to create a growth engine is gone.

A clear, carefully developed Roll-Out Plan can help to avoid this scenario.

24. Sample Roll-Out Plan A

Goal: Identify information and contact people for the key areas to support our new partnership.

1. Roles and responsibilities. For each of the areas listed below, identify the main item to be accomplished and the correct person who will be responsible:

	Item	To Be Accomplished	Contact Person
a.	Value proposition and positioning		
b.	Marketing		
c.	Sales lead generation		
d.	Qualification criteria for sales leads		
e.	Sales training		
f.	Proposals		
g.	Closing of sales		
h.	Billing		
i.	Contracts with clients		
j.	Delivery of product/service		

k.	Client support and account management			
l.	Information Technology			

2. Roll Out Questions

a.	Big Picture	What are our corporate goals with this partnership?	
		How do we keep this simple?	
		How will Company/Partner interact in collaborative areas?	
		How will each step be supported?	
b.	Systems	What systems will be used?	
		What systems must interact at Company/Partner?	
		What tools need to be developed for success within the above design?	
c.	Training	How do execute initial and ongoing training for our teams?	
d.	Marketing	How do we market the products/services to our customers and prospects?	
		What market segment is the focus of our partnership?	
		What marketing tools do we create?	

		How do we brand this?	
		How do we introduce this to our internal organization?	
		How do we keep up with ongoing communications within the organization and externally?	
	e. Sales	What portions of the Partner business/sales force will be involved?	
		What is roll out plan by sales segment?	
		How do we hold our sales force accountable for results?	
		How do we incorporate this into our current sales offerings?	
		How and what do we want to report on?	
		How do we track the pipeline?	
		How do we manage leads?	
		What is the sales commission structure and how do we pay sales people their commission?	
		What is the Sales Training schedule and plan?	
	f. Account Management	How do we handle customer service requests?	

		How will we receive, escalate and resolve client issues? (Tier 1, Tier 2)	
		How is this communicated? By whom?	
g.	Operations	How do we roll the service/product out to prospects and clients?	
		How do we on-board business – implement clients?	
		What are the points of integration?	
h.	Finance and Accounting	How do we price the products and services?	
		How are price changes managed? (volume discounts, introductory pricing, etc.)	
		What are the service details?	
		How will we bill, track and reconcile billing with our clients?	
		Who is billing the client?	
		What contract format/paperwork needs to be executed by client?	
		What is the payment structure?	

25. Sample Roll-Out Plan B

The following example of a Roll-Out Plan for "Monisure Company" is a high-level plan that lists the items to be covered in the early days of the partnership. Some of the items continue beyond the roll-out period.

Monisure Company - Partner Roll-Out Plan

Following is a plan showing how we – Monisure Company – work with and support our strategic partners.

This plan is modified based on further discussions with you, our partner. The goal of this plan is to outline the steps we follow to make sure the teams at your company and at Monisure are fully aware of the strategy, value and products we are bringing to the market.

---

a. **General Partnership Success Elements**
   - Monisure has assigned a Partner Manager to be the primary point of contact.
   - Weekly partner calls are to be held on Tuesday at (____time____). On these calls we will discuss:
     - Measurement: track sales success
     - How to maintain momentum with sellers
     - Highlight client wins
     - Quarterly sales promotion
     - Opportunities and areas for improvement
     - Tracking of scheduled dates for the roll-out and milestones.

b. **Technology Issues**

- IT teams identified to review integration and other issues.
- Business Analyst assigned to gather requirements.
- Scope of Work developed to address the necessary steps and timeline.

c. **Operations Issues**
   - Determine workflow with existing products
   - Points of integration
   - Bundling of product/service with existing ones

d. **Customer Support and Implementation Training**
   - Identify client support and implementation teams
   - Conduct in-person or webinar training
   - Provide product overview and demonstrations
   - Determine client support roles:
     o Who will support the client when they have issues and questions?
     o Tier 1 vs. Tier 2 support roles
     o Escalation processes
   - Monisure support contacts
   - Support tools
   - FAQs
   - Screen shots
   - Product demonstration links
   - Fact sheets and collateral.

e. **Sales and Marketing**
   - Clarify and state the branding and description of the products/service and company - partner relationship
   - Announce Kick-off
   - Sales process
   - Sales tools (ROI calculator, scripts, etc.)
   - Sales training scheduled
   - Collateral developed
   - Sales goals identified by sales leader

- Sales commission structure addressed
- Web site announcement and description
- New Release issued announcing the partnership
- Sales lead tracking in place using CRM system

f. **Account Manager Training**
   - Identify partner company account managers.
   - Conduct in-person or webinar training:
   - Product overview and demo
   - Value to partner company, clients, sales team
   - Pricing

g. **Current Client Communication and Training**
   - Identify partner company training contact
   - Integrate training with existing methodologies
   - Client training manual or items
   - Other support documentation
   - FAQs
   - Demonstrations and webinars

h. **Ongoing Partnership Success**
   - Maintain momentum with marketing
   - Newsletters, e-mail campaigns, webcasts, white papers
   - Implementation success
   - Implementation weekly status calls
   - Implementation tracking report to make sure all items are covered and that there is clarity about responsible parties and timelines
   - Issue resolutions, process improvements
   - Partnership Commitment
   - Dedication, sense of urgency

26. Sample Roll-Out Plan C

Sample Partner Checklist – Launch Plan

1. **High Priority**
    a. Provide Partner the link to web site and landing page where product will be described and ordered
    b. Confirm partner product access and reporting are all working as expected
    c. Product placement -- in partner's product offering
    d. Finalize where customers will access product offering
    e. Finalize what the access looks like (link, button, etc.)
    f. Soft launch / pilot
        - Determine if we'll have a soft launch / pilot.

        If yes, when: _____

    g. Full launch
        - Determine Target go-live date _____

2. **Next Steps**
    a. Marketing
    b. Introduce marketing teams
    c. Align on types of joint and individual marketing.
        - Create downloadable datasheet
        - Create one-page description of product
        - Create blurb we can put on web site about the product - one paragraph.
        - Create direct client communication – repurposing the blurb

      d. Determine joint Go To Market - GTM - Plan
      e. Training (Back into this date after soft-launch or final launch date)
      f. Determine if any Partner teams need training on our product
      g. Account management, sales,
- Give training if required
- Accounting (Back into this date after soft-launch or final launch date)
- Engage accounting teams
- Be sure it is clear what each is expecting from the other

3. **Launch Prep**
   a. Soft launch – *Pilot Program*
   b. ID pilot / soft launch customers
   c. Partner product is ready and available for customers
   d. Launch to customers
   e. Confirm partner product access, reporting, accounting *(Make sure everything is working as expected)*
   f. Full launch
   g. Launch to all
   h. Check- in to see that reporting, activity, and product usage is as expected.

4. **Post Launch Review**
   a. Weekly check-ins for the first month after launch
   b. Once per month check-in for the next few months
   c. Discuss usage, activity
   d. Pricing

e. Identify desired enhancements
f. Get customer feedback and case studies
g. Client testimonials and references

27. Announcing a New Partnership

When a new partnership is launched, it is important to issue a news release and messages announcing the relationship sent to: (a.) company associates and (b.) clients.

The internal message is often overlooked. It may be drafted by the Partnership Manager but sent from a senior executive. This can give it added horsepower.

We find this simple step can be extremely effective when rolling out new partnerships to bring awareness and clarity about the goals of the relationship. A straightforward e-mail or other communication to internal employees can simply state:

- The reason for the partnership
- Who is in charge?
- The reason for the relationship
- Where to find more information

An example of such a communication is shown on the following page. A similar type of message – but directed at clients – can be appropriate, too. Of course, this can be personalized and sent by specific account managers or others who own each strategic relationship.

What is most important is to share the news. Sending a message to internal associates and clients deserves to be included as part of the standard roll-out plan for new partnerships and alliances.

Sample Letter to Internal Associates about a New Partnership

Re: New Partnership Between Monisure and Zentow

Dear Colleagues,

As you know, Monisure is committed to bringing quality service and solutions to our clients. To support these objectives, we have entered into a new strategic partnership with Zentow Corporation.

Zentow is a leading supplier of compliance services for the construction industry. You can discover more about Zentow by visiting their web site – zentowwebsite.com.

This partnership was developed to augment our set of solutions for employers and to bring best-of-breed products to clients. Because of this relationship, we can now offer our clients in the construction industry an automated solution for financial and operational compliance and risk mitigation.

We will include Zentow's services as part of our platform to provide clients with a consistent experience. The strategic goals of this relationship include helping clients manage risk and achieve savings through administrative efficiencies.

For Monisure, we see this relationship as a way to strengthen our relationship with clients and deliver added value.

We will be having a brief company webinar about this new partnership, which I encourage you to join if your schedule allows. Also, additional information is available on our web site announcing the partnership.

Our Partnership Team has been hard at work identifying ways to accelerate our company's growth with strategic relationships.

As always, thank you for all of your efforts to build Monisure and bring terrific service to clients.

28. News Releases about a New Partnership

Having an announcement on your web site and a news release for distribution to the media sites, journalists and bloggers regarding a newly formed partnership is considered a best practice. The Partnership Manager may work with external communications, marketing or the appropriate people with both partner companies for the proper wording and message.

Following are two examples of news releases announcing a new and then an expanded partnership:

Sample News Release

Apploi and iCIMS Announce Partnership to Integrate

Hourly Job Search App and Talent Acquisition Suite

Mobile-ready hiring community joins iCIMS' growing partner ecosystem

---

NEW YORK, March 10, 2016 – Apploi (www.apploi.com), a mobile-adaptable job search app that allows hourly job seekers and employers to easily connect, today announced a partnership with iCIMS, Inc., a leading provider of innovative Software-as-a-Service (SaaS) talent acquisition solutions.

Apploi is pleased to announce an integration into the iCIMS Talent Platform, a suite of talent acquisition software tools that enables organizations to attract, screen, communicate with, and hire the best talent for their business needs. Companies who take advantage of this integration can quickly capture their hourly service and support workers through Apploi and automatically transfer them into the iCIMS Talent Platform, where recruiters can manage the hiring process from start to finish, all within in a single, cloud-based application.

"Working with the leader in the talent acquisition market helps improve the process for those in the working groups faced with the highest unemployment rates," said Adam Lewis, CEO of Apploi. "We have always been committed to helping bridge the gap between those looking for hourly service and support positions, and companies looking to hire great team members. Now through integration with iCIMS, we have taken another step toward this goal."

"With mobile and tablet usage among job seekers showing a staggering 60 percent increase, as well as shortages of candidates in many industries across the United States, an integrated system to seamlessly connect hourly job seekers with employers via mobile devices is greatly needed in today's employment landscape," said Michael Wilczak, senior vice president, strategy and corporate development of iCIMS. "Through our partnership with Apploi, we add one of the most well-developed mobile job searching apps to our growing partner ecosystem to help our customers solve their hourly hiring challenges," Wilczak concluded.

About Apploi

Apploi is a mobile-first platform for job seekers and employers to easily connect. The job search app is available on the Google Play and App stores, as well as on the web, and is focused on the retail, restaurant, hospitality and service industries. Apploi works with over 5,000 companies across the United States, from Fortune 500 companies to small and mid-sized businesses. Users can apply to jobs directly through the app and use its interactive features like video and audio responses to show their personality and passion far more effectively than on a traditional resume.

About iCIMS, Inc.

iCIMS is a leading provider of innovative Software-as-a-Service (SaaS) talent acquisition solutions that help businesses win the war for top talent. Scalable, easy to use, and backed by award-winning customer service, iCIMS enables organizations to manage their entire talent acquisition lifecycle from building talent pools, to recruiting, to onboarding, all within a single cloud-based platform that is connected to the largest partner ecosystem of HR technologies in the industry. Supporting more than 3,200 contracted customers, iCIMS is one of the largest and fastest-growing talent acquisition solution providers. To learn more about how iCIMS can help your organization, visit http://www.icims.com.

Sample News Release
Qlik and Keyrus Expand Global Strategic Reseller Partnership

After years of successful partnership, companies now extend analytics offering to nearly twenty countries

May 4, 2016

ORLANDO, Fla - Qlik (NASDAQ: QLIK), a leader in visual analytics, and Keyrus, an international player in the fields of Data Intelligence, Digital, and Consulting on the Management and Transformation of enterprises, today announced the expansion of their global strategic partnership driven by strong client demand. A Qlik partner for almost 10 years, Keyrus and Qlik have agreed to stronger go-to-market and sales commitments, with Keyrus now reselling and licensing Qlik solutions in nearly 20 countries, including France, Switzerland, Belgium, Luxembourg, Spain, the United Kingdom, United Arab Emirates, the United States, Canada, Brazil, China, Morocco, Tunisia, Algeria, Israel, and South Africa. Keyrus' competency in delivering end-to-end Business Intelligence (BI) services and solutions, combined with Qlik's modern, platform-based approach to BI and analytics, will widen the scope, scale, and value of solutions offered to clients in the retail, supply chain, healthcare, and sales and marketing segments.

"Qlik is the preferred vendor of many of our clients for visual analytics solutions," said Eric Cohen, CEO of Keyrus. "This is because over the years Qlik has perfectly met the requirements of so many diverse companies across different industries. From this experience, we at Keyrus are convinced that this expanded strategic partnership with Qlik is the right step forward in ensuring that we can continue to accelerate our joint engagements and serve our current and future clients. With Qlik's powerful visual analytics platform, our global expertise and reach, we will deliver increased value and high ROI to clients across the world."

Both companies will jointly bring these solutions to market to deliver a self-service analytics culture to an extensive set of enterprise-level clients. Keyrus is also creating a Qlik Center of Excellence and plans to extensively train its workforce in the next 12 months to capture the business opportunity around building Qlik solutions and taking them to market. This will also help its clients continue on their journey to becoming more data-driven, agile enterprises.

"Our relationship with Keyrus is creating competitive advantages for our customers by helping them to deploy end-to-end, data-driven solutions for their BI and analytics needs," said Toni Adams, Senior Vice President, Partners and Alliances, Qlik. "With the strategic and global nature of our partnership, we are committed to building on our strengths – Keyrus' rich experience in delivering end-to-end solutions and services and Qlik's unique platform approach to visual analytics. Together, we are focused on building and delivering the foundational elements for the deep insight necessary to make the promise of agile business a reality."

About Keyrus

An international player in consulting and technologies and a specialist in Data and Digital, Keyrus is dedicated to helping enterprises take advantage of the Data and Digital paradigm to enhance their performance, facilitating and accelerating their transformation, and generating new drivers of growth, competitiveness, and sustainability.

About Qlik

Qlik (NASDAQ: QLIK) is a leader in visual analytics. Its portfolio of products meets customers' growing needs from reporting and self-service visual analysis to guided, embedded and custom analytics. Approximately 39,000 customers rely on Qlik solutions to gain meaning out of information from varied sources, exploring the hidden relationships within data that lead to insights that ignite good ideas. Headquartered in Radnor, Pennsylvania, Qlik has offices around the world with more than 1700 partners covering more than 100 countries.

29. Segmenting the Audience for a Roll-Out

Sometimes new partnerships may be rolled out to the full client base of each company as part of the launch plan. Alternatively, a segment of the client base or market can be targeted in the beginning of a new partnership. This can be before everything is set and final decisions are made about how to enter the market. The segmented approach warrants consideration.

Basically, the idea of the segmented approach is to layer in different groups (customers, prospects and internal resources) and create use cases along the way. This helps prove the partnership has merit and paves the way for expansion.

Maybe you are just unsure about the value of the partnership and how the market will receive it. This situation can give rise to using a segmented approach versus a full scale roll out.

A segmented launch is perceived as lower risk and lower cost. Using this approach can help the Partnership Manager overcome resistance, too. Let's say the company is busy with many other projects at the same time a new partnership is available. It is hard to get the attention and resources needed to move it forward. The Partnership Manager may be able to find a segment of the business or a market sector that will allow the partnership to get started, in a smaller way and requiring fewer resources and dependencies.

While your market research shows it makes sense and client interviews support doing the partnership, you still might have some questions. Maybe you need clarity about the positioning or presentation of the product. Or maybe your doubts are centered on pricing. Introducing the partnership to a market segment can help you better understand the positives and negatives and let you refine the partnership before committing to a full launch.

Ways to Segment

- ✓ **Prospects Only.** In the initial roll-out a partnership may be introduced to *prospects* instead of a company's existing customers. This approach – albeit rather conservative – can be a smart way to go in some circumstances. It is seen as a way to lower the risk level and reduce the cost of a new partnership. By focusing on prospects, the existing business derived from current customers is not put at risk. Existing customers are not exposed.

  Usually this approach involves fewer resources, too. For example, sales people are involved and trained about the value of the partnership and products involved. But account managers responsible for retaining current clients may not be included during the roll-out or introduction period. Of course, they would likely become involved as sales occur.

- ✓ **Existing Clients Only.** In some cases, a new partnership is introduced to existing clients *only* and not to prospects.

✓ **Other Segmentation Approaches.** The Partnership Manager can also consider segmenting the market by geography, industry type, size of client, products presently used and according to other elements.

The possibility of segmenting the market for the roll-out of a partnership is worth considering. Partnership Managers can discuss the pros and cons with sales leaders and other stakeholders to help reach the right decision.

With a new partnership, the layered or segmented approach also gives the Partnership Manager a chance to evaluate what it is like working with the other team. Understanding the ins and outs of the company and preferences can be beneficial.

Of course, the risk with a layered approach is that the sales results will probably be smaller. Sales are likely not to be realized as quickly as compared to a larger roll-out. Consequently, managers can discount the worth of the partnership or lose interest in the relationship.

If a segmented approach is chosen, be sure to let everyone know the game plan. For example, explain that the partnership is starting with a sub-set of clients to test the offering and determine the best go to market strategy.

Also, it may be wise to share a timeline for expanding the partnership so it is clear to all stakeholders what the broader plan is for the relationship. This will help keep in mind that larger results are possible and the use cases developed in the segmented phase can contribute to the established long-term goals and greater success.

30. Training

Training is an important element for new and established partnerships. What's more, structure is needed to carry out the training and make it a success. Training should not be treated as a trivial item and conducted, ad hoc, when needed. Instead, a deliberate training plan with a well-organized approach showing when the training will be done and the content to be covered will go a long way in bringing success to your partnerships.

When we talk about training here, we are generally thinking that training should be a two-way street. That is, each partner training the other on their respective services and products. There may be situations when the training is one-way. Company X may be reselling Company Z's product and the agreement is not reciprocal. In that case, the training would be conducted by Company Z to inform Company X about the value, features and other aspects of the product or service.

Training is a way to gain awareness and build confidence about each of the partner's products and services. It is not a one-time event. Routine, regularly scheduled training sessions will help be a continuous reminder about the relationship and how to achieve the stated goals.

Different groups, such as sales, account management, operations, can be the audience. And the discussion items may vary for each session. The Partnership Manager, working with other business unit leaders, might want to schedule a couple of sessions at a time - even if the next one is a few weeks or months in the future. This sends the message that the partnership is solid and we will keep talking about different aspects of the offering.

A best practice is to treat these training sessions with a great deal of professionalism. Have a crisp agenda, relevant collateral material and be well prepared to discuss all points. This can have the effect of gaining support and respect. A loose session without structure or purpose diminishes the importance and seriousness of the partnership. If anyone thinks it is a waste of time, that notion can easily spread and degrade the whole program.

On-line and recorded learning tools should be embraced. Recorded sessions and narrated PowerPoint presentations are easy to create and can be reviewed by stakeholders at their convenience.

Diligent follow-up after the training is well worth the effort to reiterate key points and address any issues that were raised. Following these steps will help strengthen the partnership.

There are too many instances where a partnership is announced, a quick training meeting is held and there is little or no follow-up. Refresher training is absolutely essential. People are busy and they forget. New people join the company who are not aware of the partnership. They need to be trained, too.

Partnership Managers must make training a part of their approach to having a structured and successful relationship.

Having a prepared training PowerPoint or outline ready to share is a best practice so your colleagues can get a sense of the content.

Sample Sales and Account Management Training

Training of Sales Associates and Account Managers at both companies is usually a top priority for Partnership Managers. Of course, these are the folks who can introduce the alliance, its goals and offerings to customers and prospects and make the partnership thrive.

In many cases, there is unrealized potential that training and explaining can help capture.

The message should be very clear and direct: *How the partnership adds value for you, your customers and your prospects.*

Below is a sample training outline – a framework - for Sales and Account Managers.

1. **How do you benefit from this partnership?**

    - Partners can make introductions for you to new opportunities and help with current ones.
    - Expand your relationships. Partners can help with outreach/strategy for target accounts. Tap *Network Intelligence.*
    - Insights, market and competitive intelligence to prepare for meetings and calls. For example, information about key people at companies you are

calling on, current initiatives, priorities, budget details, culture and style, operations.
- Realize new points of view and suggested approaches as supplied by partners.
- Help with your pipeline. Validating opportunities, pushing stalled deals.
- Assistance with growth within an account.
- Help with contract renewals.
- Regional events. Increased attendance and introductions to make events a success.
- Benefits from association. Being connected with reputable partners can amplify credibility.

2. **What can you do to further the Partnership?**

   - Partnerships are a "Give/Get Relationship."
   - Look for ways to assist our partner with introductions and assistance.
   - Know the details/values/use cases for the partnership and integration.

3. **Be prepared for calls and meetings with customers and prospects**

   - Understand the business, integration and service model.
   - Review mutual customers and case studies.

4. **Keep the partnership in mind**

- Listen for opportunities and signals that your customer or prospect may have a need that can be satisfied by the partner.
- Share information you gather from the field with the Partnership Management Team to communicate to the partner company.
- Be aware of, and sensitive to, potential conflicts. For example, if the partner introduced you to bring a specific product to their customer, focus on that product. If the partner has another product that is the same, or similar, to one you sell, do not try to displace the partner. This will be seen as inappropriate and potentially disruptive to the partner's business relationship with the company. *Any risk of creating animosity should be completely avoided.*
- Update the CRM and Partner Portal used for tracking account activity.

Managing Strategic Partnerships

31. Managing the Strategic Partnership

Following the roll-out phase, a partnership requires continued attention. In fact, sometimes the Partnership Manager gets excited about setting up a new partnership and the existing, more mature relationships are neglected.

Structure during the *management phase* of a partnership keeps the relationship moving forward and can help avoid problems. To champion a partnership requires being tuned into the different components that can make it a success and avoiding pitfalls that occur all the time in business.

Having a Project Plan in place, keeping it current and communicating the progress being made can help the partnership stay on the prescribed course. It keeps everyone aware of how the partnership should fit together and the steps that are necessary.

Significant effort and resources went into developing the partnership. It is only right to pay attention and apply structure to maintaining the relationship and continuing the excitement and momentum that everyone had when the agreement was signed. Proper management will also help to promptly identify and deal with problems that may arise.

Following is a sample Strategic Partnership Project Plan which is meant to be used as a document to keep the relationship front and center and help to ensure the relationship produces the expected results.

The idea of this Project Plan is to have a clear document (A Charter) to guide project execution and project control. It is used with all stakeholders to see the goals, steps, timeline and other relevant information.

In the following chapter is a sample Project Plan. You may want to insert columns to the right for different time intervals to help track progress of the partnership.

A best practice is to review the Project Plan each month with the involved parties to see how the project is progressing. This helps identify any speedbumps that have gotten in the way and open items.

Like all documents in the structured partnership approach, the Project Plan is meant to be a living document that is updated and modified over time.

32. Sample Strategic Partnership Project Plan

Element	Description of Element	Company	Partner Owner
Commercial Agreement	Summary		
Time Line	High level view of relationship development/attainment of business goals		
Pipeline	Ongoing assessment of performance. Monthly/Quarterly update and evaluation of performance. Continuous improvement recommendation.		
Rollout Process - Joint and Internal Preparation for Launch Readiness Assessment	Key stakeholders are informed about the partnership and have participated in developing awareness of their teams.		
Readiness Function Stage	Summary description listing features of the partnership.		

Process Fundamentals - Key Inputs	Determine best path to realizing goals of the partnership: sales, marketing, operations, IT.		Training of Stakeholders and learning items/videos
Training	Training curriculum for each partner - dependent on partner. Organizational awareness plan.		Dependent on roles.
Website: Company offering and information	Should note relevant positive attributes.		Branding, press releases, competitive positioning, etc.
Marketing/ Communications	Co-branded materials.		What is joint value proposition to marketplace?
Compensation	Comp plans for participating sales personnel and account managers.		
IT - Technology	IT may need to process/approve any system configuration for the system functional requirements to support the partnership. APIs available and used.		

Reporting and Billing	Must be able to report Partner sales revenue, calculate internal and external commissions.		
Lead assignment process - Enabling Sales	Internally developed process to assign, allocate and track Partner leads within existing systems - with connection to above reporting functionality		
Finance	Pricing, billing, etc.		
Onboarding Implementation Service	Management of new clients		
Sales	Sales will support each Partner within its structure.		
Executive Sponsorship	Key stakeholders. How are issues escalated and resolved?		

33. How to Use Value Inflection Points

In the lifecycle of strategic partnerships, there are key drivers that disproportionately create or destroy ue. These are Value Inflection Points. They exist in all partnerships and are identified by Partnership Managers to deliver optimal results.

Value Inflection Points are when value is produced or erased in an outsize way. By recognizing inflection points, Strategic Partnership Managers can apply resources to the right activities and elevate the rate of success. Instead of spending time equally on various parts of partnership development and management, managers spend time where the greatest value is likely to be produced. If you don't recognize an inflection point, and act on it, your results may decline.

David Thompson, Chief Alliance Officer with Eli Lilly and Company, has studied inflection points and how they impact partnerships. Speaking at the 2017 Association of Strategic Alliance Professionals (ASAP) Global Alliance Summit, Thompson shared that the value chain relating to partnerships is not linear. He said managers can control Value Inflection Points and deliver better returns by deploying alliance resources to support the right activities. The first step is to fully understand the value drivers that are present in an organization's channel program.

For example, a company may significantly increase the success of partnerships by having a strong product launch. The aware manager will use knowledge of this Value Inflection Point to emphasize elements involved in the roll-out process and associated Go to Market activities. With that in mind, time is spent carefully planning the launch and executing on those items.

The late Andy Grove, co-founder and former CEO of Intel, spoke and wrote a great deal about inflection points. In an address at the Academy of Management Annual Meeting in 1998, Grove said: "An Inflection Point is when a change in the curvature takes place, and depending on the actions you take in responding to this challenge, you will either go on to new heights or head downward in your prosperity as a firm."

In sum, knowing and capitalizing on Value Inflection Points are a great way to achieve strong results in partnerships.

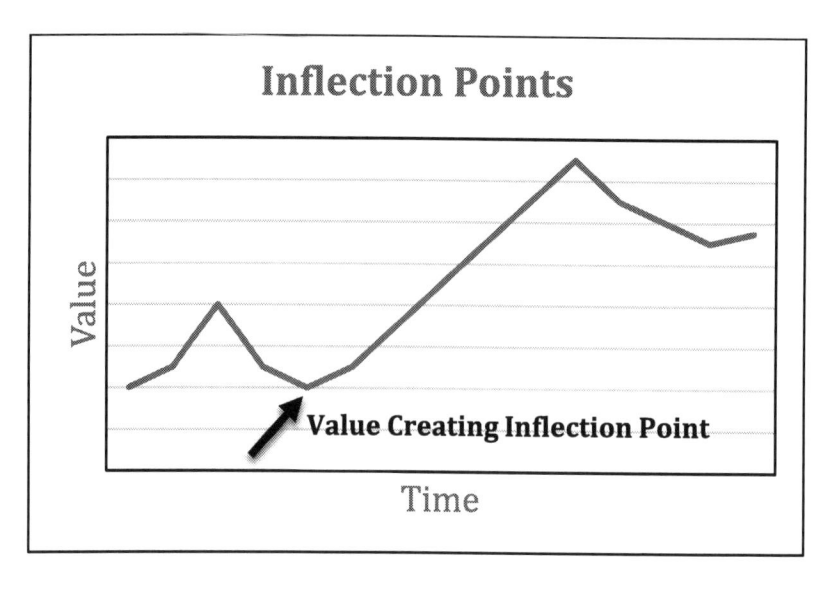

Inflection Points

Value Creating Inflection Point

34. Scorecard for Evaluating Partnerships

A recommended practice is to have regularly scheduled communication between the managers of the relationship on both sides. A weekly or bi-weekly call to stay in close touch and review progress and open issues works well in many cases.

It can be useful to have a standard scorecard to periodically measure the strength and health of the partnership.

The scorecard can serve as the basis for a quarterly or semi-annual review and discussions with key stakeholders about the status of the partnership. It gives managers a standard way to look at the relationship and coordinate adjustments that may be required. *What is working? What needs improvement?*

Routinely tracking key metrics as part of these sessions can be useful. It helps to avoid scrambling to pull the data together when preparing for a quarterly or annual review.

A sample scorecard for this purpose is shown on the following page.

We find conducting this review on a quarterly schedule works well.

Partnership Scorecard – Company A and Company B

Period Covered: _____

1. New clients and sales - wins	
2. Number of presentations made	
3. Significant new prospects	
4. Variance compared to projections	
5. Existing account penetration (upsells, cross-sales)	
6. New product/ business development or competition activities	
7. Level of customer satisfaction (Net Promoter Score)	
8. Marketing and sales efforts achieved/planned	
9. Training achieved/planned	
10. Service – operations issues	

35. User Conferences: The Partner Manager's Role

In a strategic alliance, there may be opportunities to participate in a Customer Conference or User Conference - hosted by your partner.

With large companies, these can be four-day, lavish affairs with thousands of participants. Of course, smaller firms have functions that are more in line with their size. More recently, they have become virtual events.

Participation may include having a speaking role, being a sponsor in an exposition area, attending sessions and meeting clients. In our experience, there can be meaningful value in support of the partnership with these events. The value is found in several areas:

- Showing your partner that you support them and their clients;

- Gaining exposure to more people at the partner company, including executive leaders;

- Visibility to customers;

- Lead generation;

- Reinforcing the relationship in the eyes of your partner, clients and other partners in the ecosystem.

Like everything in business, there is an associated cost. And the question always arises: *Is that cost worth the benefit?*

As a Partnership Manager this can be tricky. We have seen where the partner manager owns the partner relationship, but spending money to participate in a User Conference may come from the sales and marketing budget. This can cause friction. It can also be a gift to sales in the form of lead flow and new sales activity.

The best way to overcome any friction and to have these events be seen as positive opportunities is for the Partnership Manager to consider these steps:

a. Obtain information about the event as soon as it is available. The host will generally publish a prospectus with detailed information about the schedule, the profile of attendees (titles, size of companies represented), cost, etc.

b. Share the available content internally.

c. Get data from the host and other past attendees you may know. This may be other partner or customers. You can often get a feel from others if the events are worthwhile.

d. Share those insights internally.

e. Work with sales, marketing and account management to determine if attending is a good investment.

f. Track results. If you have attended in the past, how many leads were generated at prior shows? How many of those leads turned into closed sales?

In many cases, the Partnership Manager can use these events as a way to underline the importance of strategic alliances to the organization. And they are a great way to strengthen the relationship with sales and marketing. (Your work got them into these shows.)

36. Customer Lifecycle Communication

When a partnership is in place, there are *mutual customers*: those customers that were referred by your partner.

The Partnership team can take responsibility for sharing information about mutual clients with appropriate people at the partner company which referred that business to you. This takes some work. But it can be helpful in being identified as a strong partner, enhancing communication and expanding the alliance.

We have used a Customer Lifecycle Event list as shown below to consider the best times to communicate with your partner about the status of mutual clients. This exercise can be useful to put structure in place.

Essentially, think about the key events in the customer lifecycle that are most relevant in your business and the type of alliance. Then work with your internal team, such as client success or account management, to develop an easy, standardized way to advise your partner of the progress or status of the relationship at these points in time. We refer to this communication as the Touchpoint.

An example of a Customer Lifecycle Event Communication Schedule is shown on the following page.

Customer Lifecycle Event Communication Schedule

Customer Lifecycle Event	Touchpoint	Example
Contract Signed, Implementation Complete and Go-Live Occurs	Communication to Account Manager or Sales Person	- Go-live date. - Products or services covered. - Data integration planned. - Insights about the relationship.
After Action Review Summary	Communication to Account Manager or Sales Person	- Feedback from client based on the After-Action Review call that takes place after each new customer launch project.
Customer Satisfaction Surveys and Annual Business Review Results	Communication to Account Manager or Sales Person	- Account Manager does an annual business review with clients. - Results to be shared including satisfaction survey results.

| Contract Renewal Preparation | Communication to Account Manager or Sales Person | • Contract renewal prep.
• Renewal preparation is usually done 6 months before expiration. |

37. Annual Audit of Partnerships

Besides the quarterly scorecard and associated meetings to track the status of partnerships, an annual audit may be desirable, especially for major partnerships. This can be a constructive process to identify and celebrate wins, serve as a reminder of the partnership with leadership and zero in on areas that need work – mid-course corrections.

An annual audit brings structure to the partnership and allows the stakeholders to pause, set some time aside to review the state of the union and come up with suggestions.

It can reveal that a major overhaul of the relationship is needed - or just minor tweaks to enhance certain aspects of the partnership. If things are not working and there is no desire to make the partnership succeed, it could be time to sunder the relationship. If things are starting to erode but the parties see value and want the relationship to succeed, then this is a good opportunity to identify steps to right the ship.

In the course of an annual audit, items may be uncovered that serve as a cautionary note for stakeholders. For example, a new trend in the market, competitive forces or changes in personnel within a partner company can suggest refresher training is needed.

The annual audit serves as a great tool to figure out how to adjust course and overcome barriers. In addition, the audit can be forward-looking. It can identify business changes that may be coming in the future. Maybe a new product is planned or a partner is preparing to enter a new segment of the market.

Identifying how the partnership can support such planned changes can be reviewed as part of the audit.

Along with the audit should be an action plan to address the findings and point out what will be done going forward.

One approach with the annual audit is for each partner to complete a brief questionnaire in advance and then have a meeting to review the responses. An action plan can be developed collaboratively after that meeting takes place with commitments on next steps.

It is suggested that the questionnaire be kept short and simple. A sample Annual Partnership Audit questionnaire is shown on the following page.

	Annual Partnership Audit Period Covered: _____ Prepared by: _____	
a.	Assess the current strength of the partnership and the trend over the past year.	
b.	Growth of the partnership in the past year.	
c.	Annual Revenue and Number of Customers.	
d.	Strategic importance to our company and customers.	
e.	How are the partners working together? The cultural fit and strategic match and interaction of the partners.	
f.	Assess communication between the partners and the ability to reach decisions.	
g.	Are internal stakeholders receiving proper training and being made aware of the partnership?	
h.	Is the service delivery meeting expectations?	
i.	Do clients understand the partnership and the products or services offered?	
j.	Are additional resources needed to achieve success? What kind of resources might help?	
k.	What are one or two areas which can use improvement – and what are the suggested plans for improvement?	

Once the Annual Audit is completed, the Partnership Managers for both companies should review and discuss the findings. They will agree on an action plan and the appropriate follow-up steps.

Then it is a best practice to share the findings with others. This should be a compact summary. The audience may include, for example, senior leadership and business unit managers.

Sharing this information:

- Identifies successes and challenges;
- Serves as a reminder to management about the partnership;
- Explains the structured process followed for evaluating partnerships;
- States the action to be taken based on the annual audit;
- Clearly presents the way forward;
- Reinforces the strategic goals of the relationship.

38. Pricing, Compensation and Payments

With strategic partnerships, pricing and payments are a critical factor. And they should be reviewed over time as the partnership develops.

Of course, the fundamental issue is how the revenue will be shared by the participating partners. Often, there is a split between the parties based on sales. The revenue sharing may vary by product and the level of work being done by each party.

In a situation where one partner is taking responsibility for sales and client support and other services, there is a reasonable expectation that they will receive a higher portion of the revenue than if they are merely referring clients to the other company to follow up and close the deal. In the latter example, the partner may receive a referral fee - a flat amount - for customers recommended to purchase a partner's product or service. This may be described in a Joint Marketing Agreement or a Cooperative Marketing Agreement between the parties.

If new products are developed by the partners and then sold in the market, this arrangement can be covered by a Joint Development Agreement and the compensation of the partners should be addressed in that agreement. Joint Development Agreements are often used to clarify what Intellectual Property (IP) of each partner is being used to create the new product and who owns the new IP that is developed.

Other pricing and payment issues to consider when designing a partnership include:

- How long will the payments continue?
- What is the official start date for when payments begin?
- What is the official end date when payments stop?
- Which partner will be responsible for invoicing and collections?
- When will payments be made?
- How is pricing changed?
- What are the payment terms?
- How will earned revenue be tracked and reported? Is there a standard report for this purpose?

It is always best to have the relevant pricing and payment items clearly addressed and agreed to by both partners.

39. The Partnership Manager's Role

Just as structure is critical for the success of partnerships, having a clearly defined description of the Partnership Manager's role within an organization can be useful. It allows for clarity about what the position entails and the scope of duties.

In Appendix 4 we have included several descriptions of the role of Partnership Managers as a reference and to illustrate ways companies think about such positions. These descriptions are from actual job postings aimed at recruiting Partnership and Alliance Managers for quality companies.

Eli Lilly and Company is widely regarded as being on the cutting edge of alliance management. In the Q3 2017 issue of *Strategic Alliance* magazine, published by the Association of Strategic Alliance Professionals (ASAP), Gary Butkus and Kerri Randel Charles, alliance management professionals with Eli Lilly, wrote about the role of the Partnership Manager. The outstanding article titled *"Building Reputation: Establishing and Strengthening the Reputation of Your Alliance Management Organization,"* gives insights about tools used at Eli Lilly to promote and maintain the company's alliance program. The authors call out the importance of the Partnership Manager and that all alliance professionals must develop a steadfast reputation:

> Whether you are part of a large alliance management team or your firm's sole alliance professional, how you conduct yourself and how you are perceived influences how your partners view you. It is your reputation.

Writing in the November 2013 issue of *HR West* magazine, Jack Pearson, an alliance management expert and former President and CEO of the Association of Strategic Alliance Professionals (ASAP), beautifully described the Partnership Manager Role:

> Like most disciplines, alliance management is both an art and a science that requires both hard and soft skills. At the core of any alliance management pro's competencies is a deep understanding of the industry in which your company operates, as well as your own organization's overarching objectives and strategy. This person needs to monitor industry trends, changes in partner organizations, and his or her own company's behavior and understand immediately how internal and external developments positively or negatively affect the organization and the partnership itself. This includes anything from a partner's acquisition that instantly creates a competitive situation (and possibly a conflict of interest in the partnership), to the appointment of a new alliance manager by the partner, or a shift in emphasis away from a particular product or service by your executive management team.

Core Skills of an Alliance Professional

Those overseeing alliances should be adept at applying several tools, methodologies, and skills that have been developed specifically for the alliance management profession over the years. They should know how to construct a governance structure replete with steering and operating committees as appropriate, and rules of engagement tailored to the respective corporate cultures of each partner. Good alliance professionals should also utilize health checks and other internal survey tools to gauge the well-being of the alliance, as well as the satisfaction of both parties. Seasoned alliance veterans know how to select the right metrics to regularly assess the partnership's effectiveness, whether it is hard figures such as revenue, leads generated, or products shipped, or less tangible measures such as adherence to schedules and quality and timeliness of information shared.

It takes experience to interact with employees of another organization as if they were your own colleagues on a day-to-day basis. Obligations, expectations, goals, and dynamics of a partnership change in the face of our rapidly-changing business world, and they continue to evolve over the lifetime of the alliance. It is a different animal to coordinate with an ecosystem of partners to adjust to new circumstances. Not only do you need to master the aforementioned proprietary tools, you must also be able to influence without the benefit of direct authority over stakeholders that, say, project managers might have over their teams.[11]

---

[11] Jack Pearson, *"Alliance Management: A Strategic Discipline," (HR West, November 2013), pp. 18-20.*

Having structure in your alliance program – and in defining the role of the Partnership Manager and team members – will help clarify the goals of partnerships and the value delivered.

40. Summary

It has been our privilege to share these thoughts with you. Our primary goal in these pages has been to describe some of the ways structure can enhance a partnership through three key phases:
- *Choosing*
- *Roll-Out*
- *Management.*

The specific components of your partnership program will be determined by your type of business and other factors. To achieve the full potential from your partnerships and alliances, the right measure of structure can become an essential ingredient.

As you move forward, we hope additional structure can be included in your partnerships and help you reach your goals.

And we hope structure can assist in keeping you on the path to success.

41. Description of the Appendices

We have included as supplemental material at the end of this book several items that might be useful to Partnership Managers.

Appendix 1	Mutual Referral Agreement	Used when two partners refer each other's products or services.
Appendix 2	Referral Agreement – Unilateral	A one-way referral agreement. One partner refers or sells the other company's products or services.
Appendix 3	Mutual Confidentiality Agreement	An agreement for each side to treat the material and information shared as confidential and not to disclose that information.
Appendix 4	Sample Job Descriptions	Several sample job descriptions describing the duties of Strategic Partnership Managers.

Appendix 1- Mutual Referral Agreement

MUTUAL REFERRAL ALLIANCE AGREEMENT

Our Company and Acme

This Mutual Referral Alliance Agreement, dated _____, 20__, is entered into by and between **OUR COMPANY**, a provider of _____, a Delaware corporation ("Our Company"), and **Acme Corporation**, ("Acme") a _____ company. In consideration of the mutual promises made herein, the parties agree as follows:

RECITALS:

A. OUR COMPANY and Acme provide certain services and technology solutions in connection with *(insert type of business)*; and

B. Both parties wish to introduce the other party's solutions and services to its clients and prospective clients. For example, Acme wishes to introduce certain OUR COMPANY's solutions to clients and OUR COMPANY wishes to introduce the ___ *(specify the type of services)* ___ services to clients and prospective clients, as appropriate.

NOW, THEREFORE, the parties agree as follows:

1. **Services:** OUR COMPANY and Acme will put forth their best efforts to provide services, as described in the applicable schedules hereto, to prospects and clients referred by the other party.

2. **Referral Arrangement:** A "Referral" is defined as a Referral Form completed and submitted by one party, for a qualified potential customer of the other party ("Prospect") where the referring party is required to facilitate the introduction via a meeting or a conference call or other appropriate means, such as by e-mail.

3. **Acme Responsibilities:** Acme agrees to facilitate the promotion and sale of OUR COMPANY services to Acme's clients and prospective clients, where deemed appropriate, as described below.

   a. Acme web-site to include the OUR COMPANY marketing description.
   b. Acme will support at least one marketing effort every six months, such as a newsletter article, e-mail campaign, webinar, etc.
   c. Acme will provide OUR COMPANY with sales and marketing support and training regarding the company's products and services to introduce those products and services to OUR COMPANY clients and prospective clients, as appropriate.
   d. Acme will provide electronic marketing materials for OUR COMPANY's use.
   e. Acme will provide sales training for the OUR COMPANY employees.
   f. Acme will refer qualified leads to OUR COMPANY for follow-up.
   g. Acme will promote the OUR COMPANY products and services to its clients and prospective clients when appropriate.

4. **OUR COMPANY Responsibilities:** OUR COMPANY agrees to support the promotion and sale of OUR COMPANY services to Acme's clients as defined below. Also, OUR COMPANY will refer clients and prospective clients, as appropriate, to Acme for the introduction of the company's products and services.

   a. OUR COMPANY web-site to include the Acme marketing description.
   b. OUR COMPANY will support at least one marketing effort every six months, such as a newsletter article, e-mail campaign, webinar, etc.
   c. OUR COMPANY will provide Acme with sales and marketing support and training regarding the OUR COMPANY products and services to introduce those products and ser-

vices to Acme clients and prospective clients, as appropriate.
- d. OUR COMPANY will provide electronic marketing materials for Acme's use.
- e. OUR COMPANY to provide training for the Acme's employees.
- f. OUR COMPANY will refer qualified leads to Acme for follow-up.
- g. OUR COMPANY will promote Acme's products and services to its clients and prospective clients when appropriate

5. **Referral Registration Submission:** For each Prospect, Acme and OUR COMPANY must fully complete and submit to the other party a Referral Form in a format substantially similar to Exhibit A and Exhibit B attached hereto (the "Referral Forms").

6. **Referral Registration Acceptance and Qualification:** OUR COMPANY and Acme shall accept or refuse such referral registration within ten (10) business days after receipt of the Referral Form. OUR COMPANY and Acme may refuse such Referral at their reasonable discretion, based upon their prior or then-current marketing activity and existing contacts or business with such Prospect. If, within six (6) months following the date of acceptance of the Referral Form by the other party, the Prospect purchases service(s) identified in the Referral Form and becomes a client (a "Referred Client"), then OUR COMPANY or Acme shall pay the other party a referral fee as provided in this agreement.

7. **Referral Fees:** Referral Fees will be paid to Acme and OUR COMPANY by the other party based on service specific revenue collected during the first year of the contract and in accordance with the applicable schedules attached hereto. No Referral Fees will be paid for any conversion, integration or customization revenues; third party revenues; and training or professional services revenues. Referral Fee(s) can be adjusted if there is a client specific business need and both parties mutually agree to the adjusted Referral Fee.

Any changes to the Referral Fee will be documented in the client specific Referral Form.

8. **Referral Fee Payment:** Referral Fees shall be paid to the other party forty-five (45) days after the monthly close based on revenue collected during the preceding month.

9. **Services and Client Support:** Both parties agree to provide the services in a professional manner and to provide adequate support to the clients of its services. Both parties will sell their services to the other party's clients, will enter into a contract with them and will invoice any fees for their services to the client directly, unless mutually agreed by the parties in certain situations such as to accommodate specific client requirements where a client desires a consolidated invoice for the services supplied by both vendors.

10. **Pricing:** Both parties reserve the right to price their services at their own discretion and without the express or implied consent of the other party.

11. **Term:** This agreement will be in force for three (3) years from the date of signing and shall automatically renew for successive one-year terms unless either party provides the other with notice of termination. This agreement may, however, be terminated at any time, by either party, with or without cause, with 90 days written notice. In the event of termination, each party will pay all referral fees due the other party on sales made and invoices submitted while this agreement was in force and will pay referral fees as provided in the applicable Schedules. The parties will not be obligated to pay referral fees based on sales made after termination of this agreement.

12. **No Agency:** Acme is not an agent or employee of OUR COMPANY and shall have no power to bind OUR COMPANY. By the same token, OUR COMPANY is not an agent or employee of Acme and shall have no power to bind Acme. Requests for services submitted by Acme will be accepted or rejected by OUR COMPANY, and re-

quests for services submitted by OUR COMPANY will be accepted or rejected by Acme.

13. **Names and Trademarks:** Both parties agree not to use the other party's name or trademarks for any listings, advertisements, publications, handouts or similar promotional items without the prior written approval of the other party.

14. **Confidential Information:** "Confidential Information" means all valuable or potentially valuable information, whether communicated in oral, written, electronic or other form prior to or after execution of this Agreement, either furnished or made available to either party by the other party ("Owner"), in connection with this Agreement, including, but not limited to, all consumer information, any investor, financial, commercial, marketing, sales, technical or scientific information (including without limitation all patents, copyrights, trademarks, service marks, trade names and dress, and applications relating to same, trade secrets, software, code, inventions, know-how and similar information), and any and all other business information.

    Any Confidential Information acquired or received by either party (the "Recipient") in the course of this Agreement will not be disclosed or transferred to any person or entity other than to employees of a party. Confidential Information received under this Agreement will be treated with the same degree of care and security as each party uses with respect to its own Confidential Information, but not less than a reasonable degree of care. The parties agree to use Confidential Information only for the purpose of performance of this Agreement and to make no copies except as necessary for performance of this Agreement.

    "Confidential Information" does not include information which (i) is or becomes generally available to the public other than as a result of disclosure by the Recipient, (ii) was known by the Recipient at the time of disclosure of the information without any obligation of confidence, and that knowledge is evidenced by reasonable proof, (iii) was or becomes available from a source other than the Owner if the source was not legally bound to maintain the confidentiality of the information, or (iv) the Recipient independently develops without use of or reference to the Confidential Information.

15. **Applicable Law:** This Agreement shall be construed in accordance with, and its performance governed by, the laws of Delaware, without regard to its conflict of law principles.

This Referral Agreement constitutes the entire agreement between the parties hereto.

OUR COMPANY   **Acme Corporation**

Signature	Signature
Name	Name
Title	Title
Date	Date

SCHEDULE 1
Referral Fees

1. Referral Fees paid to Acme by OUR COMPANY

Referral Fees will be paid to Acme by OUR COMPANY in accordance with the referral fee defined below.

<u>OUR COMPANY Solutions</u>

Acme will be entitled to receive a referral fee of 10% of the first-year client revenue collected by OUR COMPANY from registered clients.

2. Referral Fees paid to OUR COMPANY by Acme

Referral Fees will be paid to OUR COMPANY by Acme in accordance with the referral fee defined below.

<u>Acme Services</u>

OUR COMPANY will be entitled to receive a referral fee of 10% of the first-year client revenue collected by Acme from registered clients.

EXHIBIT A
Acme Referral Form to OUR COMPANY

Referral Registration Submission	
Acme sales rep name, title, phone email	
Prospect company name and headquarters address	
Prospect contact name, title, phone and email	
# of company employees	
Describe your relationship with the prospect	
OUR COMPANY service(s) of interest	☐ Software X ☐ Software Y
Comments	
Submitted by:	
Name	
Title	
Date	
☐ I understand that by clicking this box, the above entry of my name serves as my electronic signature.	
Referral Registration Response	
Acceptance	
☐ Yes ☐ No Service X ☐ Yes ☐ No Service Y	
Referral Fees 10% of first year subscription revenue	
Responded by:	
Name	
Title	
Registration Date	

EXHIBIT B
OUR COMPANY Referral Form to Acme

Referral Registration Submission	
Acme sales rep name, title, phone email	
Prospect company name and headquarters address	
Prospect contact name, title, phone and email	
# of company employees	
Describe your relationship with the prospect	
OUR COMPANY service(s) of interest	☐ Service X ☐ Service Y
Comments	
Submitted by:	
Name	
Title	
Date	
☐ I understand that by clicking this box, the above entry of my name serves as my electronic signature.	
Referral Registration Response	
Acceptance	
☐ Yes ☐ No Service X ☐ Yes ☐ No Service Y	
Referral Fees 10% of first year subscription revenue	
Responded by:	
Name	
Title	
Registration Date	

Appendix 2 – Referral Agreement - Unilateral

REFERRAL AGREEMENT

THIS AGREEMENT ("Agreement") is made as of (the "Effective Date"), by and between _____ a Delaware corporation with a place of business at _____ ("_____") and _____, a _____ corporation, with its principal place of business at _____ ("Referring Party"); individually a party (a "Party"), collectively the parties (the "Parties").

WITNESSETH:

WHEREAS; it is desired that the Referring Party promote XX products that are listed herein and refer potential customers to XX; and,

WHEREAS; XX agrees to provide the Referring Party marketing assistance, training and product demonstration support related to the marketing and referral of its products, all as more fully described herein; and,

WHEREAS; it is desired that the Referring Party market and promote the following proprietary XX products and services ("Products"):

- YYY
- ZZZ

and,

WHEREAS, Referring Party and XX desire to enter into an Agreement whereby the Referring Party shall be allowed to market and promote the above listed products of XX, refer potential customers to XX and where XX successfully executes an agreement for its product based on the marketing efforts of the Referring Party, compensate the Referring Party for its marketing efforts, all as more particularly described and subject to the terms and conditions described herein.

NOW, THEREFORE, the Parties hereto agree as follows:

1. **Customer.** For the purposes of this Agreement, a customer ("Customer") is defined as a business or affiliate unit thereof that is being referred (the "Receiving Party") by the Referring Party due to the marketing efforts of the Referring Party and that also meets the following criteria:

   (a) is not currently and/or has not been a customer/client of XX within the last twelve months; and,

   (b) was referred during the term of this Agreement; and,

   (c) the marketing referral was regarding the XX Products; and,

   (d) was referred in writing by a sales manager or salesperson of the Referring Party to a XX sales manager (or a sales manager's designee) and accepted as a prospect by same; and,

   (e) the Referring Party formally introduces the prospect to XX and further provides reasonable assistance to XX in assessing the qualification level of the prospect (i.e. interest level, budget, product fit, decision makers and time frame), such reasonable assistance to be determined and accepted by the individuals identified in this subsection (d); and,

(f) the referred prospect executes an agreement with XX for a license or right to use the specific XX Product(s) that was referred, and the execution of this aforementioned agreement occurs within one (1) year of the date of the acceptance of the marketing referral by XX, such acceptance date as defined in subsection d and e above.

2. **Marketing Services and Customer Agreements.** The Referring Party shall use commercially reasonable and good faith efforts to market XX's products and to refer Customers to XX. The Referring Party may introduce the XX products and/or services as an independent third-party brand and as an adjunct to the sale of the Referring Party's own products and/or services as expressly provided herein. XX will reasonably share information requested by the Referring Party as to the progress and status of sales activities for a given Customer. In the event a Customer wishes to enter into a new relationship with XX for the receipt of the XX products and/or services, XX shall enter into an agreement directly with the Customer. The Referring Party shall not be a party to any such Customer agreement nor shall the Referring Party be responsible for either Party's compliance or non-compliance with the terms and conditions of such Customer agreement. The Referring Party shall not be responsible for any costs or losses suffered by XX if any Customer should decline XX offers. For the term of this Agreement, the Referring Party's territory for marketing referrals to each other under this Agreement shall not be limited to any specific country or countries.

3. **Marketing Assistance.** In order to facilitate effective co-marketing as described in this Agreement, each Party may provide to the other Party marketing materials in the reasonable quantities and types requested. These may include newsletters, bulletins and other similar marketing materials and online demos for its products and/or services. Each Party shall retain the ownership, right, title and interest in and to any such marketing materials provided to the other Party and neither Party will take any action to undermine or chal-

lenge the other's marketing materials. Any marketing materials provided under this Agreement shall be used solely to facilitate the marketing endeavors as expressly set forth in this Agreement. No Party is authorized to make any changes or alterations to the other Party's marketing materials or any other written information pertaining to offerings of that Party's products and/or services provided under this Agreement. Neither Party shall make any news release, published announcement or advertisement concerning the other Party, the relationship between the Parties, this Agreement or a Customer without the prior written consent of the other Party. Neither Party shall use the other Party's name, logo or any mark in any marketing or other material without the other Party's prior written consent.

4. **Trademarks.** Neither Party shall, pursuant to this Agreement or otherwise, have or acquire any right, title or interest in or to the other Party's trademarks or trade names. Each Party's use of the other Party's trademarks shall be under the other Party's trademark policies and procedures in effect at the time of usage and as may be amended from time to time. Neither Party shall have the right to use any trademark of the other Party except to refer to the other Party's products or services.

5. **Term and Termination.** The term of this Agreement shall commence on the Effective Date and continue in effect until one year after the effective date of this agreement (the "Initial Term"). Thereafter, this Agreement shall be automatically renewed for additional one-year periods (each additional period a "Renewal Term"). Either Party may elect to terminate this Agreement at any time by providing the other Party with a sixty (60) day prior written notice if its intention to terminate. The effective date of expiration or termination of this Agreement is referred to in this Agreement as the "Termination Date".

6. **Payment for Marketing Efforts.** XX shall compensate the Re-

ferring Party for the referral of Customers due to Referring Party's marketing efforts as follows:

XX shall pay the Referring Party a marketing referral fee as defined and set forth below (the Referring Party Marketing Fee") for each Customer referred to XX by the other Party under the terms of Section 1 above.

The Referring Party Marketing Fee shall be equal to two and a half percent (2.5%) of the service and/or license fees actually collected by XX from each Customer who uses a XX Product as a direct result of the Referring Party's marketing referral to XX as set forth herein, excluding however, value added tax or any other similar tax which XX shall be legally obligated to impose and any amounts due to XX's licensors and/or vendors of third party products incorporated into or bundled with XX Product(s). The Referring Party's Marketing Fee shall continue to be paid to Referring Party with respect to a Customer for one (1) year from the effective date of the first billable period the Customer is contractually obligated to pay a service and/or license fee to XX, provided this Agreement has not been earlier terminated.

Notwithstanding anything set forth in this Agreement, under no circumstances shall XX be required to pay the Referring Party a Referring Party's Marketing Fee for any service and/or license fees that it does not collect. All payments of the Referring Party's Marketing Fee's shall be paid in arrears within thirty (30) days of the end of the calendar quarter for which XX collected the applicable service and/or license fees. Notwithstanding the termination of this Agreement, Referring Party's' right to receive the Referring Party's Marketing Fee for any Customer referred to XX prior to the Termination Date of this Agreement shall continue for a period of the lesser of six (6) months from the Termination Date, the end of the Referring Party Marketing Fee one year obligation, or until such time as the Customer is no longer contractually obligated to pay XX for the XX

Product and XX is therefore no longer collecting a service and/or license fee from that Customer for the XX Product.

7. **Warranties.** Each Party represents and warrants to the other that in performing its obligations under this Agreement it shall comply with all applicable federal, state and local laws and regulations, and that it is free of any contractual obligations that would prevent it from entering into this Agreement. BOTH PARTIES AGREE THAT THEIR RESPECTIVE PRODUCTS OR SERVICES ARE BEING OFFERED AS IS, AND NEITHER PARTY MAKES ANY WARRANTY AS TO ITS USE OR PERFORMANCE. EACH PARTY DOES NOT AND CANNOT WARRANT THE PERFORMANCE, INFORMATION OBTAINED, OR RESULTS CUSTOMERS MAY OBTAIN BY USING THAT PARTIES PRODUCTS OR SERVICES. THE WARRANTIES CONTAINED IN THIS AGREEMENT ARE IN LIEU OF ALL OTHER WARRANTIES, EXPRESS OR IMPLIED, INCLUDING BUT NOT LIMITED TO THE IMPLIED WARRANTIES OF MERCHANTABILITY AND FITNESS FOR A PARTICULAR PURPOSE.

8. **Liability.** In no event shall either party be liable for any loss of profit or any special, incidental, consequential or punitive damages. Only in the event of infringement shall either Parties liability under this Agreement exceed in the aggregate those monies actually paid to the other pursuant to this Agreement for the three (3) months preceding the event giving rise to the liability.

9. **Attorneys' Fees.** The prevailing Party shall recover from the non-prevailing Party its reasonable expenses, court costs and reasonable attorneys' fees in any litigation arising out of this Agreement.

10. **Severability.** In the event that any provision of this Agreement (or any portion thereof) is held to be invalid, illegal or unenforceable, the validity, legality or enforceability of the remainder of this Agreement shall not in any way be affected or impaired here-

by.

11.   **Force Majeure.** Neither Party shall be liable or deemed to be in default for any delay or failure in performance under this Agreement or interruption of service resulting directly or indirectly from acts of God, or any causes beyond the reasonable control of such Party.

12.   **Notices.** All notices given under this Agreement shall be in writing and delivered or transmitted by fax to the address set forth below or such other address as a Party may from time to time specify in writing to the other Party. The addressees to whom notice are initially to be sent are as follows:

        If to <u>XX</u>:   If to Referring Party:

13.   **No Third-Party Beneficiaries.** No customer or employee of either Referring Party or XX or any other person or entity not a party to this Agreement shall be entitled to assert any claim hereunder. In no event shall this Agreement constitute a third-party beneficiary contract.

14.   **Governing Law.** This Agreement shall be deemed entered in and governed by the laws of the State of _____.

15.   **Assignment.** This Agreement shall be binding upon and inure to the benefit of the respective successors and assigns of the parties. However, neither party may assign this Agreement, in whole or in part, without the prior written consent of the other party.

16.   **Waivers.** The waiver by any Party of a breach of any provision, agreement or covenant of this Agreement by the other Party shall not operate or be construed as a waiver of any subsequent breach of the same or any other provision, agreement or covenant by such other Party. Except as otherwise provided herein, provisions of

this Agreement may be modified, amended or waived only by a written document specifically identifying this Agreement and signed by a duly authorized representative of each of the Parties.

17.   **Entire Agreement; Amendments.** This Agreement is intended by the Parties to be the final expression of their agreement and is a complete and exclusive statement thereof. This Agreement may be amended only if such amendment is in written form and executed by both parties.

18.   **Construction.** This Agreement shall be construed fairly, in accordance with the plain meaning of its terms, and there shall be no presumption or inference drawn against the Party drafting this Agreement in interpreting the provisions hereof.

19.   **Counterparts.** This Agreement may be executed in one (1) or more counterparts, each of which, when so executed and delivered, shall be deemed to be an original and all of which, together, shall constitute one (1) and the same Agreement.

20.   **Confidentiality.** During the course of performing under this Agreement, one Party (the "Recipient Party") may have access to customer lists, computer software, business methods or other technical or business information which is not generally known and which is proprietary to the other Party (the "Disclosing Party"), its customers or to other parties affiliated with the Disclosing Party ("Confidential Information"). Specifically, the Recipient Party agrees to treat as Confidential Information all information concerning the Disclosing Party's customers and customers' employees and employee recruitment programs, and the Disclosing Party's products, services, pricing, business plans and marketing strategies, or of which the Recipient Party is otherwise made aware in connection with performing under this Agreement. The Recipient Party agrees to maintain all such Confidential Information in confidence during the term and after termination of this Agreement, and not to disclose or permit

access by any third party to any such Confidential Information, except to the extent disclosure is expressly permitted by the Disclosing Party. The foregoing obligations shall not extend to any information which the Recipient Party can establish (a) was, at the time of disclosure, generally available to the public through no fault of the Receiving Party, (b) was in the Receiving Party's possession on the Effective Date and was not obtained from the Disclosing Party, (c) was lawfully received from a third party who rightfully acquired it and did not obtain it in violation of any confidentiality agreement, (d) was independently developed by the Recipient Party without violation of any provision of this Agreement, or (e) was required to be disclosed by a court or other governmental authority and reasonable notice was given to the Disclosing Party. The obligations set forth in this Section shall survive the termination of this Agreement.

21. **Independent Contractor.** This Agreement is not intended to nor does it constitute or create a joint venture, partnership, or other relationship of any kind except as specifically described in this Agreement. Neither Party shall have authority to bind the other, except to the extent specifically described by the terms of this Agreement or otherwise in writing. Each Party shall be and shall remain an independent contractor and shall be solely responsible for all its employees and other obligations arising in respect of its performance of this Agreement. Except for any representations that may be contained in any marketing and advertising materials that may be prepared jointly and agreed to by both parties, or as otherwise expressly agreed to in writing, neither Party shall be authorized to make representations to any third party regarding the other Party or its products or services. The business relationship between the Parties shall be non-exclusive and shall not restrict either Party from doing business with any third party.

22. **Indemnification.** XX, at its own cost and expense, shall indemnify, defend and hold harmless Referring Party and its respective affiliates, subsidiaries, employees, representatives and

agents against any claim, suit, action, expense or other proceeding brought against Referring Party based on or arising from any claim that any information provided by XX to Referring Party infringes upon the intellectual property rights of any third party or is otherwise related to the performance of XX' obligations under this Agreement. Referring Party, at its own cost and expense, shall indemnify, defend and hold harmless XX and its respective employees, representatives and agents against any claim, suit, action, expense or other proceeding brought against XX based on or arising from a claim that any information delivered to XX by Referring Party infringes upon any intellectual property rights of any third party or is otherwise related to the performance of Referring Party obligations under this Agreement. Further, the Parties agree to indemnify each other from any general cause of action.

23. **Audit.** Each Party shall maintain complete and accurate books and records of any Customer transactions of relevance to this Agreement, including invoices and proof of Customer payment thereof during the term of this Agreement. Each Party shall have the right, at its own expense but no more than one (1) time each calendar year, to have a certified independent auditor examine, upon reasonable prior written notice and during dates and times mutually agreed upon by the Parties, the other Party's books and records relating to the other Party's compliance with Section 6 of this Agreement.

24. **Ownership.** Nothing in this Agreement shall be construed as granting a Party any rights in the other Party's products and services. Each Party shall retain all title, patent, trade secret, trademark, copyright and other proprietary rights in its products and services.

25. **Other Transactions.** Nothing in this Agreement shall prevent Referring Party or XX from engaging in any type of business transaction with any third parties.

The undersigned have caused this Agreement to be effective and binding unto the Parties as of the Effective Date.

XX	YY
Signature	*Signature*
Name	*Name*
Title	*Title*
Date	*Date*

Appendix 3- Mutual Confidentiality Agreement

MUTUAL CONFIDENTIALITY AGREEMENT

This Agreement, dated _____, 20__, by and between _____ ("_____") located at _____, a _____ corporation, and _____ located at _____, a Delaware corporation.

The nature of this Transaction (as defined below) may include the sharing of Proprietary Information (as defined below) between the parties, and the parties agree to keep all such proprietary information confidential and not disclose such information to others.

1. <u>Background</u>. The parties hereto intend to engage in discussions and negotiations concerning a possible business transaction or relationship (the "Transaction"). In the course of such discussions and negotiations, it is anticipated that each party will disclose or deliver to the other party and to the other party's directors, officers, employees, agents or advisors (including, without limitation, attorneys, accountants, consultants and financial advisors) (collectively, "Representatives") certain of its trade secrets or confidential or proprietary information for the purpose of enabling the other party to evaluate the feasibility of the Transaction. The parties have entered into this Agreement in order to assure the confidentiality of such trade secrets and confidential or proprietary information in accordance with the terms of this Agreement. As used in this Agreement, the party disclosing Proprietary Information (as defined below) is referred to as the "Disclosing Party" and the party receiving such Proprietary Information is referred to as the "Recipient."

2. Proprietary Information. As used in this Agreement, the term "Proprietary Information" shall mean all information concerning the Disclosing Party (whether prepared by the Disclosing Party, its Representatives or otherwise and irrespective of the form of communication) which has been or is furnished to the Recipient or its Representatives by or on behalf of the Disclosing Party. In addition, the term "Proprietary Information" shall be deemed to include any notes, analyses, compilations, studies, interpretations, memoranda or other documents prepared by the Recipient or its Representatives which contain, reflect or are based upon, in whole or in part, any Proprietary Information furnished to the Recipient or its Representatives pursuant hereto.

3. Use and Disclosure of Proprietary Information. The Recipient and its Representatives shall use the Proprietary Information only for the purpose of evaluating, negotiating or advising with respect to the Transaction and the Proprietary Information shall not be used for any other purpose without the prior written consent of the Disclosing Party. The Recipient and its Representatives shall hold in confidence, and shall not disclose, any Proprietary Information of the Disclosing Party; provided, however, that (i) the Recipient may make any disclosure of such information to which the Disclosing Party gives its prior written consent; and (ii) any of the Proprietary Information may be disclosed by the Recipient to its Representatives and to any employees ("Affiliated Employees") of any entity which controls, is controlled by or is under common control with, the Recipient who need to know such information for the sole purpose of evaluating, negotiating or advising with respect to the Transaction and who agree to keep such information confidential. In any event, the Recipient shall be responsible for any breach of this Agreement by any of its Representatives and Affiliated

Employees, and agrees, at its sole expense, to take reasonable measures to restrain its Representatives and Affiliated Employees from prohibited or unauthorized disclosure or use of the Proprietary Information.

4. <u>Limitation on Obligations</u>. The obligations of the Recipient specified in Section 3 above shall not apply, and the Recipient shall have no further obligations, with respect to any Proprietary Information to the extent that such Proprietary Information:
   a) is generally known to the public at the time of disclosure or becomes generally known through no wrongful act on the part of the Recipient;
   b) is in the Recipient's possession at the time of disclosure otherwise than as a result of Recipient's breach of any legal obligation to the Disclosing Party;
   c) becomes known to the Recipient through disclosure by sources other than the Disclosing Party having the legal right to disclose such Proprietary Information;
   d) is independently developed by the Recipient without reference to or reliance upon the Proprietary Information; or
   e) is required to be disclosed by the Recipient to comply with applicable laws or governmental regulations, provided that the Recipient provides prior written notice of such disclosure to the Disclosing Party and takes reasonable and lawful actions to avoid and/or minimize the extent of such disclosure.

5. <u>Ownership of Proprietary Information</u>. The Recipient agrees that the Disclosing Party is and shall remain the exclusive owner of the Proprietary Information and all patent, copyright, trade secret, trademark, domain name and other intellectual property rights therein. No license or conveyance of any such rights to the Recipient is granted or implied under this Agreement.

6. Return of Proprietary Information. The Recipient shall, upon the written request of the Disclosing Party, return to the Disclosing Party all Proprietary Information received by the Recipient from the Disclosing Party (and all copies and reproductions thereof). In addition, upon any such request, the Recipient shall destroy all Proprietary Information prepared by the Recipient or its Representatives and Affiliated Employees (and all copies and reproductions thereof). Notwithstanding the return or destruction of the Proprietary Information, the Recipient and its Representatives and Affiliated Employees will continue to be bound by their obligations of confidentiality and other obligations hereunder.

7. No Representation or Warranty. Each party acknowledges and agrees that all Proprietary Information is provided without any representation or warranty, express or implied, as to the accuracy or completeness thereof. Only those representations and warranties which are made in the final definitive agreement concerning the Transaction, when, as and if executed, and subject to such limitations and restrictions as may be specified therein, will have any legal effect.

8. Miscellaneous.

a) Without the prior written consent of the other party hereto, each party will not, and will cause its Representatives not to, disclose to any person the existence of this Agreement, the fact that Proprietary Information has been made available to either party, the fact that discussions or negotiations are taking place concerning the Transaction or any of the terms, conditions or other facts with respect to the Transaction, including the status thereof, unless required to do so in accordance with Section 4(e) above.

b) This Agreement supersedes all prior agreements, written or oral, between the Disclosing Party and the Recipient relating to the subject matter of this Agreement. This Agreement may not be modified, changed or discharged, in whole or in part, except by an agreement in writing signed by the Disclosing Party and the Recipient.

c) This Agreement will be binding upon and inure to the benefit of the parties hereto and their respective heirs, successors and assigns.

d) This Agreement shall be construed and interpreted in accordance with the internal laws of Delaware, without giving effect to the principles of conflicts of law thereof.

e) The provisions of this Agreement are necessary for the protection of the business and goodwill of the parties and are considered by the parties to be reasonable for such purpose. The Recipient agrees that any breach of this Agreement will cause the Disclosing Party substantial and irreparable damages and, therefore, in the event of any such breach, in addition to other remedies which may be available, the Disclosing Party shall have the right to specific performance and other injunctive and equitable relief.

f) The term of this Agreement is two years from the date of its execution. For the convenience of the parties, this letter agreement may be executed by facsimile and in counterparts, each of which shall be deemed to be an original, and both of which taken together, shall constitute one agreement binding on both parties.

g) For a period of one year following the date of this agreement, neither party will directly and knowingly recruit or solicit any employee of the other party with whom the party has had direct contact regarding the Transaction, so long as the employee is employed by such other party. In addition, neither party will directly and knowingly induce or attempt to induce any employee of the other party with whom the party has had direct contact regarding the Transaction to terminate his or her employment with such other party. The foregoing restrictions on recruitment, solicitation and inducement shall not apply to the usage of any general employment solicitation efforts such as newspaper, radio and Internet advertising, or with respect to any employee of a party who initiates, directly or indirectly, discussions with the other party regarding potential employment.

SIGNATURE PAGE

EXECUTED as of the day and year first set forth above.

(XXX)

_____

Signature Above

By: _____

Title: _____
E-mail _____
Phone: _____

Company

_____

Signature Above

By: _____

Title: _____
E-mail: _____
Phone: _____

Appendix 4 – Sample Job Descriptions

> **Example #1**
>
> **Director of Strategic Alliances**
>
> **Stroz Friedberg**

Why Stroz Friedberg?

Working at the intersection of technology, investigations, regulatory governance and behavioral science for well over a decade, Stroz Friedberg is driven by a core purpose—seeking truth. We consider this the underpinning to our success at helping organizations find facts, manage enterprise threats, and move forward with greater assurance.

Stroz Friedberg is a leading professional services firm specialized in investigations, intelligence and risk management. To help our clients manage risks, we have assembled a collection of the brightest minds in the fields of Digital Forensics, Incident Response, Security Science, Intelligence and Investigations, Data Discovery, Forensic Accounting and Compliance. With twelve offices across the globe, Stroz Friedberg is on an exciting growth trajectory, and the size of our organization will let you stand-out and operate on the front lines as an innovative fact-finder, allowing you to showcase performance excellence and drive success for our clients, the firm, and yourself.

Position Overview

The Director of Strategic Alliances will be responsible for identifying and cultivating strategic revenue-producing partnerships and alli-

ances in conjunction with the Company's Business Unit leaders. The ideal candidate is a seasoned and successful business development executive with a strong professional network and who is able to negotiate and manage synergistic, mutually productive alliance relationships for Stroz Friedberg. This role requires a balance of strategy, design and execution to drive revenue through these partnerships. Key to the role is effective collaboration with multiple cross-functional, cross-Business Unit stakeholders and sales.
The Director of Strategic Alliances will also be responsible for assisting with strategic planning activities that support the ongoing development of the firm's long-term business plans and corporate strategy.

Core Job Functions

- Understand the Company's priority growth strategies and effectively translates strategy into actionable programs that can be implemented with existing and new alliance partners to drive revenue.
- Perform comprehensive analysis of potential and current alliance partners to develop compelling revenue producing programs that best aligns with key company growth program objectives.
- Own the process for setting and measuring key metrics to evaluate contribution to revenue as agreed with key business unit stakeholders.
- Locate or propose potential alliance relationships/programs by contacting potential new and existing alliance partners; discovering and exploring opportunities.
- Close new alliance partner agreements by coordinating requirements; developing, negotiating and executing contracts; integrating contract requirements with business operations.
- Provide the business rationale for the partnership with key business unit stakeholders to execute the programs and deliv-

er planned success metrics – with compensation tied to annual based goals and objectives.
- Establish annual business plans which define annual objectives, joint solutions and marketing programs, and field engagements.
- Measure achievement against annual revenue goals as defined by senior leadership (e.g., annual revenue, Y/Y growth, new market selection and penetration).
- Collaborate with marketing, sales and/or delivery teams to ensure company readiness and ability to drive sales; drives global implementation of the joint initiatives.
- Maintain executive level interaction with strategic alliances, customers, industry influencers, and key Stroz Friedberg stakeholders.

Required Skills

- Experience working with global alliance partners and developing strategic GTM plans around joint service offerings.
- Strong project management, time management, and organizational skills to effectively supervise projects to completion
- Track record in IT consulting, managed services, security, or similar technical industry preferred.
- Understanding of service and product differentiation and competitive strategy techniques preferred
- Excellent oral and written communication skills, superior client/executive interaction.
- Highly self-motivated individual with keen sense for converting conceptual ideas into programs that produce tangible results.
- Intellectual curiosity, ability to learn quickly, and a passion for building a best-in-class firm.
- Work proactively and collaboratively; ability to work in a fast-paced environment
- An enduring interest in the cyber security industry.

Education Required - Bachelor's degree required. MBA preferred.

Work Experience Required - 7 years of experience in Strategic Partnership/Alliances Management. Experience in Business Development or similar roles in the enterprise software and IT consulting industries welcome.

Example #2

Director, Strategic Partnerships

Websense - Austin, TX

Job Summary

Raytheon|Websense is seeking a Director of Strategic Partnerships to join the Raytheon|Websense Corporate Strategy team, reporting to the VP of Corporate Strategy. The Director will act in a business development capacity, identifying and cultivating strategic partnerships and alliances in conjunction with the company's functional leaders. The ideal candidate is an experienced business development leader with a strong professional network within enterprise cyber security software markets and is able to lead the growth of a strategic partnership pipeline, assist the company in prioritizing partnership opportunities, and manage the process from business plan to execution. The Director of Strategic Partnerships is also responsible for assisting with strategic planning activities that support the ongoing development of the company's corporate strategy and associated long-term business plans.

Essential Functions

- Ownership of an overall partnership strategy for the company which aligns with the Company's priority growth strategies
- Development and ownership of a pipeline of strategic partnerships across all areas of the product portfolio, and new growth areas
- Achieving alignment across functional organizations that are cultivating potential partnership opportunities
- Translation of partnership strategy into actionable, revenue-generating programs with existing or new partners

- Generation of a company-level partnership assessment and prioritization framework, including standardization of business case analysis
- Setting evaluation criteria for each partnership program and measuring success
- Managing new partner agreements, from negotiating scope to supporting the legal team in execution of agreement/contracts
- Work closely with Corporate Development, Product, Engineering, Sales, Marketing, the CTO office, Professional Services, and other business stakeholders
- Supporting Finance in financial planning and forecasting
- Reporting to company Executives, Owners and Board of Directors on partnership strategy and status

Education and Experience

- Bachelor's degree required; MBA preferred
- Strong project management, time management, and organizational skills to effectively supervise projects to completion
- Experience in information technology, software, or security software industries
- Previous experience in the security software market preferred; general knowledge of the security software market is acceptable given the right candidate that can come up to speed quickly on new technologies and concepts
- Demonstrated results in growing a successful partnership program
- Excellent oral and written communication skills
- Experience generating compelling business cases with actionable, measurable execution plans
- Must be highly self-motivated, able to work autonomously and in a high-pressure environment
- Strong, demonstrated qualitative and quantitative analysis skills

- Strong interpersonal skills and ability to work in matrixed organizations
- Process-oriented and driven to achieve strategic goals
- Exceptional interpersonal, written/oral/listening communications and presentation/persuasion skills
- Demonstrated analytical ability, strong knowledge of statistical analysis and modeling capability, and expertise in both quantitative and qualitative data collection techniques (including surveys, usability testing and analysis, and focus groups)
- Vendor management experience
- Proven success managing cross-functional initiatives
- Experience in global markets a plus
- Must have a passion for data and the ability to draw conclusions from complex data sets
- Highly organized and detail oriented
- Ability to multi-task and manage multiple projects at the same time
- Ability to travel about 30%.

Example #3

Director of Business Partnerships

TicketNetwork, Inc. - South Windsor, CT

Ticket Galaxy is a leading Connecticut-based, professional ticket broker selling tickets to concert, sport, and theater events around the world. As a ticket reseller, Ticket Galaxy is dedicated to offering great tickets at highly competitive prices. Ticket Galaxy's premiere customer service provides consumers with access to hard-to-get, sold-out, and discount tickets to popular live entertainment events.

The primary responsibility of the **Director of Business Partnerships** will be the establishment of new business partnerships in the worlds of live music and sports. Working through new and established industry contacts, the Director of Business Partnerships will prospect, pursue, and execute ticketing and sponsorship opportunities with concert promoters, artists, agents, and managers as well as professional sports teams and venues.

Responsibilities include:

- Growing Ticket Galaxy's exclusive ticketing partnerships in the areas of live music and sports
- Developing strategic plans to the development of new business and the maintenance of existing partnerships
- Identifying new partner prospects and actively managing a pipeline for new opportunities
- Crafting customized messaging and proposals that outline the company's distinct capabilities, service offerings and strategic goals for its partners
- Conducting pitches for prospective clients
- Attending sales conferences to promote the company's mission and brand

- Maintaining visibility, accessibility, and cultivating relationships
- Driving revenue and profitability through partnership growth.

Required Skills

- Superior interpersonal skills
- Strong written and verbal communication skills
- Excellent organizational and time management skills
- Ability to analyze new business opportunities as well as research and detect problems
- Confidence in selling, negotiating and closing sales skills
- Must be an outgoing, self-starter with a positive attitude

Required Experience

- At least 5 years of experience in the live music and sports industries, preferably some background in ticketing
- Established contacts and relationships throughout the live music industry
- At least 5 years of experience in a professional sales environment
- Experience utilizing MS PowerPoint for professional presentations

> **Example #4**
>
> **Global Alliance Manager**
>
> **Ericsson**

Ericsson Overview

Ericsson is a world-leading provider of telecommunications equipment and services to mobile and fixed network operators. Over 1,000 networks in more than 180 countries use Ericsson equipment, and more than 40 percent of the world's mobile traffic passes through Ericsson networks. Using innovation to empower people, business and society, we are working towards the Networked Society, in which everything that can benefit from a connection will have one. At Ericsson, we apply our innovation to market-based solutions that empower people and society to help shape a more sustainable world.

We are truly a global company, working across borders in 175 countries, offering a diverse, performance-driven culture and an innovative and engaging environment where employees enhance their potential every day. Our employees live our vision, core values and guiding principles. They share a passion to win and a high responsiveness to customer needs that in turn makes us a desirable partner to our clients.

Job Summary

Ericsson is driving a paradigm shift in how cloud is bought and sold in the enterprise segment thru channel partners. Ericsson is looking for an experienced Global Alliances Executive for Business Unit Cloud & IP to develop relationships with selected Global Alliance partners, across the portfolio and manage the success of our global partnership.

As a Global Alliance Manager within Ericsson Cloud, you will have the exciting opportunity to deliver on our strategy to build mind share and adoption of the Ericsson cloud marketplace and align more of our strategic alliance partners' products and services.

Responsibilities include building up the strategic relationship with one of the largest system integrators in the world, driving executive alignment, product team alignment, marketing support, along with field and channel relationships. By establishing and growing business and technical relationships, along with managing the day-to-day interactions, you will be responsible for driving profitable growth for Ericsson.

The ideal candidate will possess both a business and technical background with strong business acumen that enables them to engage at the CXO level as well as operate across and connect at multiple levels in an organization. The candidate must possess a solid sales and marketing or business development background, with a strategic focus to drive multi-year strategic plans as well as comprehensive Go-To-Market plans with the right mechanisms that drive results – aligning product management, marketing, & sales across Alliance Partner and Ericsson.

The ideal candidate will also have a demonstrated ability to think strategically and technically about business solutions with the ability to build and convey compelling value propositions.

Roles & Responsibilities

On a global basis to define product strategies, develop and execute joint sales and Go-to-Market (GTM) programs.

- Engage the *Alliance Partner* Executive leadership, Business Unit Product Managers, Marketing, and Sales channels to

create and drive revenue and margin optimized plans for both parties.
- Manage day-to-day business relationship with partner(s), oversee all aspects of the relationship and ensure regular, coordinated interaction.
- Build out future Business Globally.
- Set a strategic business development plan for target markets and ensure it's in line with the Ericsson's strategic direction. This includes developing a detailed alliance plan and establishing a process to track the progress toward goals.
- Set and manage revenue targets and work with *Alliance Partner and Ericsson sales* organizations to achieve/exceed goals.
- Solution identification and development
- Business Case development and joint go-to-market planning
- Identify specific customer segments and industry verticals to approach with a joint value proposition.
- Understand the partner's business goals and work closely with the internal development team to guide the direction of Alliance Partner's product offerings based on our market intelligence.

Qualifications

- The right person will possess 10 years of proven business development experience in the technology industry
- A minimum of 5 years working with channel partners.
- Consistently exceeds goal and key performance metrics, with hands on experience negotiating enterprise contracts, and developing comprehensive go-to-market plans with F100 companies.
- Strong presentation and communication skills; ability to articulate complex concepts to cross functional audiences and drive mindshare.
- Strong business and technical acumen, with a demonstrated track record of driving, growing and managing a partner portfolio.

- Ability to think and work creatively to develop unique joint value propositions.
- Oversee and manage joint corporate alliance agreements and their compliance, including business agreements such as Letters of Understanding, Non-Disclosure Agreements, etc.
- Effectively build strategic working relationships and develop and use collaborative relationships to facilitate the accomplishment of work goals.
- Build trust and display confidence in his or her intentions and those of the organization.
- Strong sense of ownership in his or her work.
- Excellent written, analytical and business development skills to balance strategic thinking and execution of tactical activity including the ability to communicate and present at an executive level.
- Bachelor's required and Master's Degree preferred.
- International experience preferred.

Example #5

Director, Strategic Partnerships

Accruent, Inc. - Austin, TX

The **Director, Strategic Partnerships** is a key position in the planned international growth of Accruent's Telecom business. Reporting to and in partnership with the General Manager, the Director of Strategic Partnerships will source potential partners, evaluate opportunities, negotiate contracts, oversee the launch of new programs, and manage existing partner relationships.

Essential Duties & Responsibilities

- Define and manage partnership framework and approach
- Develop the partner strategy by collaborating with all relevant functions within company
- Manage all aspects of partnerships including the contractual relationship, sales and services agreements, measures of success, reporting, etc.
- Position partners for success with internal stakeholders
- Execute industry, channel, market and competitive research and analysis to identify strategic partnership opportunities
- Develop and implement business plans with each strategic partner including sales, marketing and technical integration opportunities
- Support and drive partner influence deals with Accruent's sales force to achieve revenue objectives
- Approach potential partners to pitch value of partnerships in conjunction with the General Manager
- Perform due diligence efforts on potential partners
- Present analyses and/or recommendations
- Develop professional relationships and regular communication with partner contacts

- Lead RFP processes during renegotiation of successful partnerships
- Travel as needed, up to 50%

Knowledge, Skills & Abilities

- Bachelor's Degree
- Minimum 10 years of experience in partnership development and management
- Experience owning and managing complex, multinational partnerships
- Outstanding interpersonal skills, with a natural inclination towards relationship-building
- Stellar written and spoken communication skills; can simplify complex topics into clear and impactful summaries and presentations
- Comfortable structuring and driving analysis to identify, prioritize, and solve complex business problems through strategic partnerships
- Experience negotiating complex commercial challenges with partners
- Strong detail and process orientation; can manage competing priorities and collaborate with stakeholders in different departments
- Passionate about working in a fast-paced, entrepreneurial growth company
- Telecommunications industry and international experience preferred
- Foreign language skills a plus

ABOUT ACCRUENT

Accruent helps real estate and facilities leaders deliver long-term, world-class operational and financial performance through industry-specific suites that deliver greater customer value. Accruent's solutions are at work in more than 4,000 leading organizations worldwide, including 40 percent of the top 100 retailers, 20 percent of the Fortune 500, 45 percent of the leading universities, all of the top 4 U.S. wireless carriers, 40 percent of U.S. hospitals, and leading service providers managing more than 4 billion square feet of property. Founded in 1995, Accruent is headquartered in Austin with offices in Santa Monica, Evanston, Columbus, Pittsburgh, Boston, Vancouver and Hong Kong.

> **Example #6**
>
> **Director of Strategic Alliances**
>
> **Rapid7**

This is an ideal opportunity for an alliances or business development leader to take on a newly created role focused on impacting strategic direction and growth at Rapid7. The timing is great for this role as Rapid7 has invested heavily in building a large ecosystem of strategic and technology partners with an unmatched foundation of technical interoperability in place.

You would be accountable for identifying opportunities at technology, consulting and managed service partners to grow our visibility, product revenue & services revenue. Rapid7's product portfolio consists of the leading solutions Nexpose, Metasploit & UserInsight.

This role reports to the head of business development. Partners you could be working with may include Microsoft, Cisco, VMware, IBM, HP and Amazon.

In this role you will work with an evolving group of strategic partners to understand their business objectives, sales methodology and go-to-market efforts for the purpose of creating and delivering on a partner strategy with a compelling joint-value proposition.

Once you identify and incubate these opportunities, you'll establish ongoing objectives and metrics to closely monitor the joint go-to-market and measure success.

Key responsibilities include:

- Relationship Management – A business leader who is able to influence and nurture all aspects of the partnership. Build re-

lationships and deliver QBRs with partner executive teams, engineering, professional services, sales & marketing.
- Alliance Strategy – Ability to think strategically and analytically about their business, product, integration and technical challenges. Ability to formulate a partnership vision, strategy, and execution plan.
- Go-to-market/Demand Generation – execution on strategic initiatives, industry & partner events, joint-lead generation activities, including sales enablement. Develop internal and external-facing marketing and sales collateral to support the alliance.
- Technical Ownership – Have the technical ability to understand security, software and recognize areas of product integration and opportunity discuss product roadmaps and engage with product managers and engineers.

Required:

- Outstanding communication and relationship skills - having the ability to sell ideas and plans to internal constituents, executives, prospects, sales teams and analyst. You should also be able to motivate and drive cross-functional teams and build and sustain relationships with key influencers.
- Self-sufficient team player – Be a self-starter with a high level of energy that thrives in a high-growth environment, yet always put the team first.
- Highly Organized – detail oriented, ability to create and track metrics to measure success
- Proven experience - 7-10+ years of relevant business development experience or sales, channels, marketing, consulting firms, MSSPs or strategic vendors.

Printed in Great Britain
by Amazon

87692489R00112